THE PURE KITCHEN

THE *Pure* KITCHEN

*Clear the Clutter from Your Cooking with
100 Gluten-Free, Dairy-Free Recipes*

Hallie Klecker

Pure Living Press

Middleton, Wisconsin

THE PURE KITCHEN

*Clear the Clutter from Your Cooking with
100 Gluten-Free, Dairy-Free Recipes*

Pure Living Press

Middleton, Wisconsin

ISBN-13: 978-0-6154950-5-7   1/12 47506109

Library of Congress Control Number: 2011933710

Cover and interior design:
Peri Poloni-Gabriel, Knockout Design, www.knockoutbooks.com

Cover photographs: Dreamstime

Disclaimer: This book has been written and produced for informational and educational purposes only. Statements within this book have not been approved by the FDA. Content should not be considered a substitute for professional medical expertise. The reader assumes full responsibility for consulting a qualified health professional before starting a new diet or health program. Please seek professional help regarding any health conditions or concerns. The author and publisher of this book are not responsible for adverse reactions, effects, or consequences resulting from the use of any recipes or suggestions herein or procedures undertaken hereafter.

*To my mom, a woman I'm blessed to have
as both my mother and my closest friend.*

*You believed in me even when I did not and
inspired me to reach out and*

*take hold of my dreams with both hands.
As your daughter and your friend, I'll always
cherish your heart in mine.*

Contents

Why I Wrote This Book

My journey toward wellness began when I first eliminated gluten and dairy from my diet. After experiencing various health issues—unexplained weight loss, fatigue, digestive problems, achiness, and mental fogginess to name a few—I cut the gluten and dairy from my diet on the recommendation of a holistic health practitioner. Within a week, I felt better than I had in months. Over time, as I began living life free of gluten and dairy, I came to realize that the allergen-free products sold in the grocery store were nowhere near healthy substitutes. Most of the packaged foods hinged on refined, starchy flours, sugar, and low quality oils. I quickly discovered that the easiest and most cost-effective way to eat would start by cooking at home.

I began exploring a wide world of nutritious foods like never before. I feasted on winter squash, sweet potatoes, crunchy kale salads, spicy chicken curries, warming soups, creamy smoothies, juicy fruits, fistfuls of nuts and seeds, and whole grains like quinoa and brown rice. Life without gluten and dairy? It had loads of flavor, not to mention mega nutrition! Not once did I crave a slice of bread or cube of cheese. My diet was varied, nutrient dense, and wholly satisfying.

I'm a believer that a diet built on a foundation of whole, pure foods—foods as they are found in nature—is the healthiest around. When I set out to write this book, my goal was to emphasize a diet rich in clean, colorful foods; a diet purified of processed junk food and fortified with fresh fruits and vegetables, lean proteins, whole gluten-free grains, healthy fats, and natural sweeteners. Eat like this and you'll be well on your way to becoming your very best self from the inside out.

Purifying Our Plates

The American diet is notorious for its supersized portions, cheap and low-quality ingredients, and grab-on-the-go convenience foods. This being the case, it's no surprise that the foods that dominate our culture—packaged snack foods, high sugar breakfast cereals and bars, frozen pizzas, and processed lunch meats and cheeses—are usually nutritional "black holes," empty and void of energizing nutrients.

You'll find very few processed ingredients in this book. Eating whole foods means eating foods in their natural, unprocessed state. Remember this: the less packaging the better.

Although I would love to make every single bite of food I consume from scratch, I'm the first one to tell you that in today's world of hectic schedules and crazy lives, that's just not practical. So in these recipes, while I've tried to keep them as pure and whole foods-based as possible, you'll occasionally find ingredients such as low-sodium chicken broth, canned beans, pureed pumpkin, applesauce, or another relatively pure but packaged ingredient. Food plays a fundamental role in our society, but I don't believe life should revolve around it. How we eat should mesh with how we live. If that means taking a bit of help from the store and buying prepared broth or a box of rice noodles, then so be it.

How to Use This Book

Cooking is an art, so always feel free to unleash your creative side in the kitchen! That being said, here are a few guidelines to help you succeed with these recipes and make the most of your time.

1. Please read each recipe all the way through before starting. I've learned this the hard way, getting through half of a dessert recipe and realizing that I'm all out of eggs or that I don't have the right pan. In the long run, reading the recipe through will save you time, money, and your sanity.

2. Clean as you cook. My mom did all the cooking in our house when I was growing up, but she was *not* a good model of this rule! Somehow she managed to dirty two or three times as many dishes as were needed when she cooked. Her random and spontaneous approach to cooking is a quirky personality trait that I've grown to love about her, but really, learning to clean up as you cook will make the dishwashing job so much easier after the meal is over!

3. Use common sense. As much as I've tried to test these recipes in various climates and kitchens, food turns out differently depending on who's making it and where it's being made. Use the time estimates given in the recipes as guidelines, but don't hold too tightly to them. When something looks, smells, and feels done, it probably is. Learn to use all of your senses in the kitchen and adjust the recipes according to your tastes, preferences, environment, and equipment.

A Note Before You Cook

After months of chronic health issues before I went gluten- and dairy-free, I slipped into depression. Sick and exhausted every day, my life felt hopeless and purposeless. It was not until I changed my diet and began cooking at home that things made a turn-around. Although I didn't realize it at the time, cooking infused my life with joy again. Stirring pots of soup, baking healthy cookies, chopping up vegetables—the process of preparing my own food helped me find happiness and pleasure in my life. I found *myself*. Somehow the girl I knew as me had disappeared into the shadows of her illness. Cooking brought her to life again.

As you cook from this book, splatter its pages with oil and flour, and scribble notes in the margins, it is my deepest hope that the recipes will fill your life with joy as they do mine. If things don't go well the first time around, don't give up. Try again. And again. Life isn't perfect and neither is cooking. Take the good with the bad, strive to improve, and above all, enjoy the journey.

We have one life to live, so let's make it the best it can be, one bite at a time. 🪶

THE ELEMENTS OF PURE EATING

. . . . .

Why Eat Pure?

Before you read a word beyond this chapter or cook a single recipe from this book, I want you to remember one very important point—pure eating is not a diet. It is a way of life.

From the moment I eliminated common allergens and inflammatory foods from my diet and began feasting on whole, natural foods, I've been convinced that eating purely is one of the most powerful and rewarding lifestyle changes a person can make. As you begin your journey through this book, de-clutter your kitchen, learn the ins-and-outs of natural foods shopping, and ultimately cook your way to a purer life, you'll quickly see that purifying your diet will not just affect what you eat but also how you live. And, perhaps more importantly, how you feel.

So, pure eating. What is it? Why eat pure? Let's dive in.

Pure Eating Defined

A pure diet is one that incorporates whole, natural, colorful foods and minimizes or eliminates those that are processed and lacking nutrients. In other words, pure eating highlights foods as they are found in nature. When we eat foods in their unrefined states, our bodies are supplied with a wealth of cancer-kicking vitamins and minerals, phytochemicals, heart-healthy fats and oils, fiber, and age-reversing antioxidants.

Processed foods are void of all of the above. White bread and corn syrup don't grow on trees or roam in fields. They don't soak up sunshine, drink up rain water, root into soil, eat grass and bugs, or breathe in fresh air either. And yet, the majority of our supermarkets contain far more white flour, sugar, refined oils, and factory-farmed meats than fresh produce, organic poultry and seafood, and whole grains.

Pure eating turns the standard American diet (aptly abbreviated the SAD) on its head. When we eliminate processed foods along with common inflammatory triggers like gluten, dairy, and refined sugar from our diets, wholesome and vibrant foods like dark leafy greens, organic proteins, nuts and seeds, beans and legumes, and juicy fruits have room to take center stage.

The result? Radiant, optimal health. I wholeheartedly believe that *we are what we eat* (and drink). A dietary foundation of low-quality and high-fat proteins, sodium-laden and sugar-rich dairy products, and refined carbohydrates is no foundation at all. We simply cannot expect to thrive on processed foods.

Optimal wellness, physical fitness, and mental clarity lie in eating purely. Fresh, colorful food layered with flavor and texture is good for our bodies and the planet. That's what pure eating is all about.

Pure Food for Health

As you thumb through the recipes in this book, you'll find that they are free of gluten, dairy, and refined sugar. Why do I cook this way?

First of all, let me assure you that I don't believe gluten, dairy, and sugar are inherently bad for us if *consumed very moderately*. However, for the vast majority of people, these foods trigger an inflammatory response in the body and are difficult to digest. Far more people are sensitive to these foods than we realize. While not everyone has clinically diagnosed celiac disease or lactose intolerance (including me), many of us simply feel better when we steer clear of these foods that frequently promote inflammation. Listening to your body and feeding it what it thrives on is an art unique to every individual and one that I believe we all should practice.

What's Up with Gluten, Dairy, & Refined Sugar?

In this section you'll find a brief overview of gluten, dairy, and refined sugar, how they affect the body, and why I chose to leave them out of this book.

Gluten is a protein found in wheat, barley, rye, triticale, kamut, and sometimes cross-contaminated oats. Symptoms of gluten sensitivity vary widely in severity, ranging from mild digestive upset to intense abdominal pain, bloating, migraines, achiness, and fatigue. Sadly, millions of people experience gluten sensitivity every day without even knowing that gluten is causing their symptoms. Removing gluten from the standard American diet is no easy task. Our supermarkets boast aisles upon aisles of gluten-laden breads, pastries, cereals, crackers, condiments, snack foods, desserts, and candies. Gluten even finds its way into processed deli meats, salad dressings, corn chips, ice cream, vegan meat substitutes, and frozen entrees.

In spite of this, gluten-free products are more prevalent now than ever before. When I first went gluten-free, I tried every brand of cookie, bread, pasta, and condiment I could find, just as long as the label read "gluten-free." I quickly learned, however, that gluten-free processed foods—other than being free of the gluten itself—are still a goldmine of refined flours, sugar, unhealthy oils, preservatives, additives, gums, and empty calories.

Over the years, I have determined that the key to unlocking gluten-free lifestyle success lies not with a brand or line of products, but rather with the concept of eating whole, natural, pure foods with as little packaging as possible. For years I've feasted on fresh vegetable salads and fruits, quinoa and brown rice pilafs, spiced poultry and meat dishes, handfuls of raw nuts and seeds, and unrefined fats and oils. I've never gone hungry. I've never hankered after a loaf of bread or bowl of buttered pasta. If you nourish your body with a broad spectrum of vitamins, minerals, and phytonutrients from pure ingredients, you will likely not crave junk food.

🖋 **Dairy products** are those made from the milk of cows, goats, and sheep. The most common dairy products available to us today are cheese, butter, milk, cream, ice cream, heavy cream, sour cream, cream cheese, and yogurt.

I was gluten-free for nearly a year and a half before going dairy-free as well. While cutting the gluten from my diet made a dramatic difference in the way I felt, I still believed something was "off" with my digestion. Upon eliminating dairy products from my diet, I noticed the disappearance of stomach aches, dark under-eye circles, and sinus congestion right away. These symptoms along with diarrhea, constipation, bloating, fatigue, achiness, mucus, and headaches are a handful of the most common signs of a dairy sensitivity.

The majority of people naturally stop making significant amounts of lactase (the enzyme that breaks down and helps us metabolize lactose, the sugar in milk) around the age of two or three. For most mammals in general, the norm is to cease lactase production shortly after they have been weaned from their mother's milk. In short, I believe our bodies just were not made to digest dairy on a regular and long-term basis.

For those seeking out more information regarding the science behind dairy-free living as well as a wealth of recipes and resources, I highly recommend the book *Go Dairy Free*, by Alisa Fleming (Fleming Ink, 2008).

🖋 **Sugar** as we commonly know it comes in the form of sucrose extracted from sugarcane or sugar beets. Sugar shows up in thousands of products, everything from baked goods to tomato sauce to toothpaste. In her excellent book *Get the Sugar Out* (Three Rivers Press, 2008), Ann Louise Gittleman writes, "The average person today eats about 180 pounds of sugar per year, or around ½ pound of sugar per day. Compare this to the consumption of less than 10 pounds of sugar per year in the late 1700s and you can see that sugar consumption has risen more than 1,800 percent in the last two hundred years!" As sugar consumption has increased, so have our waistlines. Diabetes, metabolic syndrome, hormonal imbalances, breast cancer, and childhood obesity rates are rising to historically high levels.

Gittleman goes on to say that high fructose corn syrup accounts for over 40 percent of caloric sweeteners added to what we eat and drink here in the United States. "The average consumption of all corn sweeteners, including HFCS [high fructose corn syrup]," Gittleman writes, "is 83 pounds per year." Found in soft drinks, syrups, pasta sauces, baked goods, protein bars, condiments, baby food, and even infant formula, high fructose corn syrup is just as prevalent in our food supply—if not more so—than granulated table sugar.

Walk through any grocery store and you'll quickly find that most products in the aisles contain sugar in some form or another. Even food items that we don't necessarily consider "sweets" (take crackers or lunch meat, for example) are often a storehouse for refined sugar. Cereal, baked goods, ice cream, snack foods, deli meats, canned vegetables and fruits, tomato sauce, bread, yogurt—sugar is everywhere and it's making us sick.

What exactly does sugar do once it's in our bodies? Well, when eaten in excess, the effects are far too many and too devastating for me to detail in the pages of this book. However, below are a handful of ways sugar disrupts our health.

✓ Sugar can **contribute to hyperactivity**, elevated adrenaline, anxiety, crankiness, and, in children, difficulty concentrating.

✓ Sugar may cause our **saliva to become acidic**, leading to early tooth decay, poor gum health, and periodontal disease.

✓ Because sugar **decreases our bodies' sensitivity to insulin**, regular sugar consumption can lead to the onset of diabetes.

✓ Sugar may **age the skin** by altering the structure of collagen in skin cells.

✓ Sugar can **increase fluid retention** in the body, causing facial swelling and abdominal bloating.

✓ Because **sugar dehydrates us**, high-sugar foods may lead to dizziness and headaches or migraines.

✓ Sugar has the ability to **increase metabolic disorders** in healthy people and promote a host of **degenerative diseases**, many of them life-threatening.

Why give up gluten, dairy, and refined sugar if you don't have symptoms of a sensitivity? Say you're already feeling great. Is there a chance you could feel even better? Absolutely! Many of the people I've met through teaching cooking classes and workshops over the years have not eaten entirely gluten-, dairy-, or sugar-free. Still, they found that when they eliminated these foods or at least cut back on them significantly, they felt more energized, less achy, and much healthier overall.

Eliminating gluten, dairy, and sugar from your diet—whether you have to or want to—is not at all limiting. In fact, I find it to be one of the most liberating lifestyle changes a person can make. Clearing out digestively-taxing dairy, cutting back on refined grains and sweeteners, and replacing them with colorful whole foods will revolutionize the way you eat and live.

The Seven P's of Pure Eating

1. **Prioritize Cooking.**

   I'm a believer that you can't eat purely unless you make it a priority to cook your own food. Period. Restaurants, no matter how healthy they claim to be, almost always add far more salt, fat, and sugar to the food than the average person would use at home. When you prepare your own food, *you* control the quality of the ingredients you use. *You* control the portion sizes you serve and eat. *You* hold the reins of what you're putting into your body.

2. **Plan, Plan, Plan.**

   Even if you're not a "planner," please: learn to love planning! It will become your best friend. Armed with a meal plan for the entire week or just a few days, you can shop for food more efficiently and economically. Sticking to your list of pure, healthy foods leaves little room for wandering into the aisles and piling junk food into your cart.

3. Pay More, Eat Less.

Choose quality over quantity. This is a tough concept for us westerners to wrap our heads around. The United States is known for its love of monstrous portions, cheap food prices, and bigger-is-better mentality. Training yourself to appreciate high-quality and often more costly food but enjoying less of it will take time, but the rewards are worth it.

4. Paint Your Plate.

Treat your plate like a canvas. Strive to add as many colors to your dinner plate as possible. The broader your spectrum of colors, the greater variety of produce you'll eat and the more phytonutrients you'll consume.

5. Patrol Portions.

Even the healthiest foods, when eaten in excess, can become unhealthy. Over the years, our views of proper portions sizes have become inflated. I'm not a weight loss specialist and don't believe in counting calories. What I do believe in is self control and eating for your body's unique make-up. Tune into what foods make you feel the best and focus on those. Eat until you're satisfied, but not full to bursting.

6. Pleasure Matters.

Eating food is a communal, ancient experience that should be enjoyable! Cooking and savoring food made with our own two hands should be a pleasurable experience. In a world of fad diets and calorie counting, we've been led to believe that food is the enemy. It's what makes us fat and sick. On the flip side, when we make nourishing choices, cultivate a healthy relationship with food, and actually enjoy what we eat, food paves the way to our best, most vibrant selves.

7. Practice Presence.

Try to eat your meals at a table in the company of family or friends, instead of by yourself in front of a computer screen or drive-thru window. Connect with your food. Savor it. When you eat, take a few minutes to center yourself. *Am I hungry? What am I craving? What's singing to my taste buds today?* Practicing the art of being present—being in the moment—while you eat will help you engage with your food in a profound way.

Clearing
the Clutter

The average supermarket presents today's shopper with a problem I have come to call "ingredient overload." Walk into a random grocery store and you'll likely be met with four or five aisles of processed snack foods, another aisle devoted solely to soda and sugary beverages, a 50-foot long run of freezers stacked high with pizzas and frozen entrees, and an overwhelming selection of yogurt, processed cheese, and packaged lunch kits.

Take a closer look at the labels of those snack foods and frozen entrees and you'll uncover lengthy ingredient lists often containing upwards of 25 ingredients, many of those nearly impossible to pronounce. Colorful packaging, health-related catchphrases, and low prices lead us to believe that the box of cereal in our cart provides us with a good source of whole grains, when in reality it also supplies eight teaspoons of refined sugar and a measly gram or two of fiber. And yet, the American diet relies heavily on these packaged foods as everyday staples.

It's no secret. We are a society dominated by processed food. And sadly, I believe it is making us sick.

Now more than ever, we need to take back our health by purifying our kitchens of the nutritionally void products that clog them and fortifying our diets with whole, natural, nourishing food. In order to help you with this daunting task,

I want to provide you with a list of foods to avoid in a pure foods lifestyle and foods to include. On the pages that follow, you will find both.

A quick word of wisdom before you read on. I once led a grocery store tour with a group of women in varying walks of health. One of the women, a mid-thirties mother of two who had recently gone gluten- and sugar-free, explored the aisles of the store for a few minutes before coming back to me with a quizzical look on her face. "How do I sort through all this clutter?" she asked. I placed my hand on her shoulder and answered, "One step at a time."

The journey toward optimal health and wellness is just that, a journey. If good health were a destination complete with a road map on how to get there, we'd all be there by now, wouldn't we? It takes time to achieve most goals in life, and it is no different with healthy eating. Eating purely is not a diet. It's a lifestyle. Change does not happen overnight. Do the very best you can and you'll be doing great!

Purify: Foods to Avoid

🖋 **Refined flours and grains**: When flours and grains are refined, they are stripped of their bran and germ leaving nothing but the starchy endosperm behind. The bran and germ house the grain's vitamins, minerals, fiber, texture, and flavor, so eating them in their whole form is the healthiest option.

🖋 **Gluten**: A protein found in wheat, rye, triticale, kamut, spelt, barley, and sometimes oats (due to cross-contamination), gluten is difficult to digest for many people and offers no nutritional value. For those with celiac disease and gluten allergies, sensitivities, or intolerances, avoiding gluten is critical for their health. Many people without a clinical sensitivity to gluten, however, find that they too feel remarkably better (less achy, better digestion, and sharper mentally) when they eliminate it from their diets.

🖋 **Refined sugar**: Plentiful in everything from condiments to baked goods to lunch meats, refined sugar depletes our bodies of vitamins and minerals, robs our cells of water, contributes to the growth of cancer cells and tumors, breaks down our bones, and weakens our immune systems making us more susceptible to illness.

✐ **High fructose corn syrup**: No different than sugar, high fructose corn syrup wreaks tremendous havoc on our bodies. Like sugar, corn syrup creates a breeding ground for disease in the body and contributes to chronic conditions such as arthritis, cancer, and obesity.

✐ **Dairy**: Much like gluten, dairy is very difficult to digest for many people. Symptoms of a dairy sensitivity include sinus issues, acne and other skin conditions, digestive upset, joint pain, and chronic illness (weakened immune system). Sugar is a common sidekick to many of the dairy products in our stores today (think ice cream, yogurt, and cheesy foods), which is all the more reason to avoid it.

✐ **Factory-farmed or processed meat, poultry, and eggs:** These foods are often laced with hormone and antibiotic residues given to the animals. When compared to organic, grass-fed, and free-range options, factory-farmed meat, poultry, and eggs have been shown to contain far lower amounts of healthy fats. From an environmental and economic standpoint, avoiding these foods makes a dramatic impact on the health of our planet as well.

✐ **Farmed or overfished seafood:** It saddens me deeply that our oceans have become so infiltrated with waste, toxins, and chemicals in recent years. While seafood can, in moderate amounts, make up part of a healthy diet, it is imperative to seek out sustainable sources that carefully track the origin of the fish. Avoid farmed and overfished species, as they lack the healthy fats and other trace nutrients of wild-caught seafood. For a guide to choosing sustainable seafood, see the website provided on page 226 of the Resources section.

✐ **Packaged snack foods:** A storehouse for gluten, dairy, sugar, additives, chemicals, colorings, and low-quality fats, packaged snack foods are best left on the shelf. While there are a handful of companies

working hard to create nutritious snack items, the majority of what fills our stores should not comprise even a fraction of our diets.

𝄢 **Soy:** Controversial in its effect on health, soy products stir up a cauldron of debate among health experts. In my experience, I've found soy to be highly allergenic and an interference with the hormones of many people, especially women, when consumed in excess. Many soy foods also pack a sky-high sodium punch and are coupled with gluten.

𝄢 **Artificial sweeteners, colors, flavors, and preservatives:** It seems like every other day I'm reading a new study on how artificial anything is causing some sort of health complication or another. Engineered in a lab and not present in nature, all of the "artificials" are most certainly not whole foods. If you're staying away from packaged snack foods in general, you'll be well on your way to avoiding these nutrition bandits!

𝄢 **Hydrogenated or partially hydrogenated oils:** Again, these fats only present themselves in packaged food products. Hydrogenated oils lead to a long list of diseases and contribute greatly to diabetes and obesity. Purging them from your diet is a giant step in the right direction toward pure living.

𝄢 **Frozen entrees:** First of all, the taste of these entrees alone should drive you away! I may be a bit biased here, but I'm pretty confident that anything you make from this book will taste far better than a frozen tray of store-bought food. Plus, you'll be avoiding empty calories, excessive sodium, hidden sources of gluten and sugar, and a laundry list of food additives.

𝄢 **Anything you can't pronounce:** This is one of the best rules you'll hear when it comes to healthy eating: if you can't pronounce it, don't eat it.

Fortify: Foods to Include

Fresh vegetables: The foundation of a healthy diet, colorful vegetables are the ultimate fortifying and nourishing food. Calorie for calorie, they pack the biggest nutrient punch of all other food groups. Go nuts for veggies. Greens, root vegetables, asparagus, broccoli, cauliflower, cabbage, peas, lettuces, peppers, green beans—it's all good!

Fresh fruit: A vitamin-rich source of carbohydrates, fresh fruit warrants a place of prominence in everyone's diet. As with vegetables, fruit offers layer upon layer of nutrient density.

Fresh herbs: Packed with oxygenating chlorophyll and antioxidants, fresh herbs also add tremendous flavor to whatever you pair them with. Years ago I never gave herbs a second glance in the market, but after trying a few recipes that captured their freshness and flavor, they are now mainstays in my refrigerator.

Grass-fed, organic, and free-range meat, poultry, and eggs: Quality is everything when it comes to animal products. Choosing cuts of meat from humanely raised, grass-fed (and preferably grass-finished) cows ensures superior environmental and personal health. The same is true when choosing organic poultry and eggs from pastured chickens. Animals raised naturally in the open air with plenty of access to sunlight and grass offer dense, high quality protein.

Wild-caught seafood: Use the guide found at the website listed on page 226 of the Resources section to help you in your search for sustainable seafood. Choose wild-caught whenever possible for optimal nutrition and planetary health.

Beans and legumes: Providing protein, fiber, and satisfying carbohydrates, beans and legumes are an undervalued ingredient. Not only do they supply vitamins, minerals, and trace minerals, but the fiber in beans and legumes also supports digestive wellness.

And honestly, could you ask for a more affordable source of super nutrition?

- **Nuts and seeds:** The ultimate convenience food, nuts and seeds are staples in my kitchen. I rarely go a day without adding them to salads, throwing them in my purse for a quick snack on the run, or using them in desserts and baked goods. Supplying healthy fats along with a modest amount of protein and fiber, I consider nuts and seeds pure living essentials!

- **Whole, unrefined, gluten-free grains and flours:** When I first went gluten-free, I was upset with the poor nutritional quality of many of the baked goods on the market. Baking mixes or prepared foods relied heavily on white rice flour, cornstarch, and potato starch, offering little satisfying fiber or flavor. Then I began to discover brown rice, millet, quinoa, buckwheat, sorghum, teff and flours made from them. Their varied flavors were robust, earthy, and entirely delicious, not to mention packed with nutrition.

- **Dried fruit (unsulphured):** When that sweet tooth creeps in, don't let a package of cookies sabotage your pure eating efforts. Reach for dried fruit! It's my secret to kicking those sweet tooth cravings the minute they strike. Dates, dried Turkish apricots, and dried Black Mission figs are a few of my favorites.

- **Natural sweeteners including maple syrup, honey, agave nectar, and coconut sugar:** Instead of loading up my baked goods with refined sugar, I use moderate amounts of natural sweeteners and often fruit to lend sweetness to a treat. Agave nectar and coconut sugar in particular are relatively low on the glycemic index, meaning that they have less of a tendency to cause a spike in blood sugar levels.

- **Extra-virgin olive oil, virgin coconut oil, and grapeseed oil:** I'll be honest. I love fat. Whether it's coming from nuts and avocados, a spoonful of coconut oil, or a drizzle of olive oil, healthy fats are one of my comfort foods. Both olive and coconut oil help fight inflammation in the body, while coconut oil even has some antibacterial and antimicrobial properties as well. I don't miss butter one bit with these oils in my pantry.

🖋 **Spices and dried herbs:** My mentor in nutrition school referred to spices and dried herbs as "booster foods," and for good reason. Cinnamon, turmeric, ginger, oregano, basil, chili powder, garlic, cumin, and countless others supply dozens of anti-inflammatory properties, boost our immune systems, and help to fight cancer. From a culinary view, my recipes simply would not be the same without the influence of a well-stocked spice drawer.

🖋 **Unsweetened almond or rice milk:** Although I'm not a fan of most replacement foods for dairy (soy butter, tofu cream cheese, and the like), I have found that unsweetened almond or rice milk work well in most recipes calling for regular cow's milk.

🖋 **Unsweetened canned coconut milk:** Nothing beats a scoop of ice cream on a hot day or a creamy bowl of curry in the dead of winter. Unsweetened coconut milk, sold in a can with many organic varieties available, lends creaminess and silkiness to dishes where one would typically use heavy cream or half and half.

A Note about Meat, Poultry, and Seafood

I eat poultry weekly and beef or fish a few times per month as a dense source of high quality protein, although I try to craft the bulk of my diet around plant-based foods. I've learned to view meat as the accompaniment or side dish instead of the main attraction. For overall personal health and the health of our planet, I believe that a plant-centric diet with moderate amounts of animal protein is a conscious choice.

I completely understand that not everyone functions well or feels their best eating vegetarian, while others feel worse eating meat. Personally, I feel optimal eating a flexitarian diet that includes both plants and animals. Being in tune with your body and eating accordingly is a wise way to approach how you eat. So if, for example, you feel like adding chicken to one of the vegetarian soups in this book or eliminating it from another, I encourage you to do so.

Balanced Eating

Adopting a pure foods diet does not entail holding to a daily calorie count or scrupulously journaling what you eat. The way I see it, healthy eating is balanced eating. Enough protein today? Lots of vegetables? How about healthy fats?

When you nourish your body with a broad spectrum of vitamins and minerals from fruits, vegetables, and other plant foods, your body will receive the nutrients it needs to perform optimally and you will likely experience fewer cravings for unhealthy foods. Human bodies are remarkable creatures, all unique in their structure and constitution. Listening to your body and adapting your eating habits to meet your individual needs leads to optimal wellness.

Of course, too much of a good thing turns that good thing into a bad thing! Overeating gluten-free muffins, even if they are made with whole grains and natural sweeteners, isn't good for anyone. The same goes with fresh or dried fruit and whole grains. Too many carbohydrates of any kind, whether whole or refined, can lead to weight gain and other issues. The importance of self-control is profound. If you struggle with overeating, even of healthy foods, I encourage you to examine your relationship with food and strive to foster a healthy connection to the food you eat.

Quality of Ingredients

Quality is equally as important as quantity when it comes to healthy eating, so I want to touch on it here.

In a perfect world, we would all eat nothing but local, organic, and free-range food. As much as I would love to eat within a 100-mile radius of where I live all year long, for a good chunk of the year Wisconsin does not offer the most garden-friendly climate. The same is true for many of you, I'm sure. So in regards to eating locally, do the very best you can. Stock up on storage vegetables (onions, potatoes, squash, and the like) in the fall when they are abundant at farmers' markets, make do through the winter, and hit the markets again come spring and summer. Plant a garden if you have the space and consider learning how to can your own food.

When you shop at the grocery store, choose organic whenever possible. Fewer pesticides and herbicides on your food mean fewer in your body or the bodies of your children. Chemicals used in agriculture promote health disruptions, so avoid them whenever you can. For a list of the most commonly sprayed fruits and vegetables and those with lower residues, refer to the website listed on page 226 of the Resources section.

Lastly, I want to address the "cost conundrum." I understand that not everyone has the financial means to splurge on that organic bottle of extra-virgin olive oil every other week or those pastured eggs. Food is a very personal matter, influencing the way we look and feel as well as our budgets. Personally, I think of the grocery store as my pharmacy. Food is my medicine. So when it comes to good quality ingredients, I am willing to pay a lot of money. That's not the case with everyone and I understand that. Healthy food is more expensive, but well worth the investment in the long run.

I encourage you to weigh the costs when it comes to choosing how you eat and do the best you can. Simply becoming conscious of what goes into your body and taking a few small steps toward healthy changes is very admirable. I said it before and I'll say it again: moving toward optimal wellness is a journey that takes time and effort. Step by step, choice by choice, meal by meal. 🖋

Becoming a
Pure Foods Cook

Before you become a pure foods cook, you need to commit to living a pure lifestyle. The foods we eat affect far more than just our health and waistlines. Since ancient times, food has played a star role in our emotions, spirituality, social gatherings, family dynamics, and self-image. I'm a believer that what we eat shapes how we live.

As you transition to a whole foods diet and dive into this new way of eating and living, there are several other influential factors to keep in mind that help to lay a solid foundation for achieving optimal wellness.

1. **Exercise**. Our bodies were made to move. Being fit doesn't mean being stick thin or a gym rat, though. The way I see it, exercise should be sustainable, affordable, and pleasurable. Find a form of exercise you enjoy and that you can stick with both physically, mentally, and financially on a consistent basis. Remember, it's about being fit and active, not the fastest, thinnest, or strongest.

2. **Sleep**. Our bodies were made to sleep, too. Rest is critical for optimal health. Without it, you'll run your body to the ground. Millions of people do every single day. We're a nation of walking zombies! No matter what you say, no one can function well on five or six hours of sleep a night. Shoot for *at least* eight or more. Don't feel guilty about catching those z's, either. Sleep is one of the most natural rhythms of

life that should not, under any circumstance, be crowded out by guilt or excuses.

3. **Relationships**. I'll be the first to admit that although I'm not much of a "people person" and consider myself to be more introverted, being in the presence of others and part of a community of friends is a sure way to lift my spirits. Friendships, partnerships, acquaintances—they all have the power to boost the joy factor in our lives, in turn reducing stress and helping to ground us.

4. **Balance**. Striking the perfect harmony between work and play (or careers and family life) is no easy task, but it's one that contributes greatly to our health. Establishing balance will require different action steps for each person and their set of circumstances. Think of what your life's goals and passions are. Envision the kind of person you want to be. As you move toward balancing the various aspects of your life, remember that no step is too small.

Committing to Cooking

If there's anything you remember from this book, let it be this: **you cannot eat purely unless you make it a priority to prepare your own food.**

Choosing to eat a diet based on whole, natural foods hinges on cooking at home. Even if you make the healthiest choices possible when eating at restaurants or take-out joints, you're missing the point. Cooking unites us to our food in a unique, primal way that's simply irreplaceable. Taking the time to prepare the food you consume with your own two hands will connect you to the source of your nourishment and give you a deeper appreciation for the ingredients that are helping to sustain your life.

I completely understand that people are busy. Schedules are crazy. Workdays are long. Parents are burned out. Although it may seem like taking a few minutes to slow down and cook a healthy meal is just a waste of our valuable time, I believe that the process is actually quite therapeutic and stress-reducing. You don't have to be a gourmet chef spending hours in the kitchen every night to be a pure foods cook. You simply have to be committed to eating well and engaging with your food.

How do you make this achievable in your busy life? We've come to my favorite subject: planning.

The In-and-Out of Planning

These four words can transform how you eat or feed your family: learn to meal plan!

Although it may seem old fashioned to plan out meals for the week, the fact is, it works. A meal plan gives you the bird's-eye-view for those few days of what you'll need to shop for and how much time you'll need to allot to cooking. The plan can be as clearly defined or as roughly sketched out as you want it to be. You can plan for just a few days or an entire week. Do what works best for you.

Start by determining how many days you'll want to plan for, taking into consideration your schedule and how you like to shop (one store, five different farmers' markets, etc.).

Then comes the fun part. Hit your favorite cookbooks, websites, blogs, magazines, and personal archives for recipes and ideas of what to make. Meal plans offer plenty of opportunities to work in easy, tried-and-true meals as well as new recipes. Decide if you want to include three meals a day or just evening meals. As you plan, consider the following:

% **The weather**. If it's a sizzling summer week, you obviously won't feel like eating Moroccan Sweet Potato & Lentil Stew! But grilled burgers with Creamy Kale Salad might be just the ticket.

% **Your family dynamics**. If you have children, think about how you can involve them in the shopping and cooking process. Chances are they'll be far more likely to eat healthy foods if they have had a chance to help prepare them. If you live by yourself, meal plans can still be excellent tools for healthy eating.

✑ **Your schedule**. We all love Julia Child, but seriously. Dive into those recipes on weekends or rainy days when you have the time, not on a busy weeknight! Pardon the pun, but try not to bite off more than you can chew. Remember that pure living is about finding joy and pleasure in the process of cooking. The last thing I want you to do is turn the concepts of planning and cooking into stressors.

Make a list of all the ingredients you'll need for what's on your plan. And here's the challenge: stick to your list! Buy what you need, leave the rest at the store. It'll still be there for you next time. Sticking to your list will save you the precious commodities of both money and time in the long run.

As you get into the swing of planning, feel free to tweak, adjust, and experiment along the way. Take time to find what works for you, your family, your schedule, and your budget. Before you know it, you'll be a pure meal planning pro!

Charming the Picky Palate: Cooking for Kids

I can't tell you how many people I've met over the years who tell me that their kids high-tail it in the opposite direction at the mere sight of a vegetable. As much as we'd love to believe that kids will eat whatever we put in front of them, the truth is, they don't. So how do we fuel up our little ones with pure, nutritious food without facing World War III at the dinner table?

A few tips to think about:

✑ Get kids involved. This is huge. Kids are far more likely to eat that floret of broccoli if they helped to cook it or even grow it. Make meal time synonymous with family time.

✑ Designate a weekly "theme night." Maybe it's Tomato Tuesday or Salad Sunday. Focus on themes that incorporate healthy foods and a bit of fun as well.

✑ Involve kids in the planning process. As you meal plan, bring your kids on board. When they see a meal on a schedule in writing and

set in stone, they'll probably be more likely to just go with it rather than put up a fuss.

🖋 Enlist kids to make their own lunches. When I was in elementary school, my mom began to give me full reign over what I put in my lunch box. Because she always stocked the refrigerator with healthy foods like fruit, cut up vegetables, proteins, and a few treats such as homemade cookies and applesauce, making healthy choices was easy for me. When I look back on it, she actually had the say on what went into my lunch box, just in a very creative, sneaky way!

🖋 Use the "three-bite" rule. Encourage children to take at least three bites of a new food before deciding whether or not they like it. And if it gets a thumbs-down, keep trying. It can take up to seven times for a child's palate to "warm up" to a new flavor profile.

🖋 Cook by color. Literally! Have your kids pick out a color for the day— maybe it's red, yellow, or orange—and then try to make and eat as many natural foods in that color category as possible. Sure, a yellow day might be filled with lots of bananas, summer squash, and bell peppers, but hey—it's all pure and healthy!

🖋 When in doubt, chill out. There are going to be days when kids just won't eat what you want them to. Pick your battles, do what you can, and move on. Remember that tomorrow is a brand new day full of fresh starts and new beginnings.

Lessons in Label-Reading

When you begin eating pure and natural foods, shopping for ingredients can feel like trudging up a mountain with bricks tied to your feet. Grocery stores are cluttered with thousands of products competing for our attention and appetites. Gluten, dairy, sugar, low-quality oils, excessive sodium, preservatives, artificial colors, and more weave their wily way into the foods we buy. In this section, I hope to educate you on how to sort through the clutter in the store and walk out with a cart full of nutritious, healthy food. It *can* be done!

First of all, let's talk about gluten, dairy, refined sugar, and the foods you'll commonly find them in. These are not exhaustive lists, but they give you a good starting point of what to look for.

SOURCES OF GLUTEN

✓ Anything made with wheat, rye, barley, triticale, kamut, spelt, or cross-contaminated oats

✓ Barley malt or barley malt syrup

✓ Some artificial colorings and flavorings

✓ Extracts made from grain alcohol

✓ Flours, breads, cereals, chips, crackers, cake mixes, and pastas

✓ Semolina

✓ Sauces or condiments

✓ Hydrolyzed protein or texturized vegetable protein

✓ Modified starch or food starch

✓ Wheat germ oil

✓ Soy sauce

✓ Spices that contain anti-caking agents

✓ Starch made from glutinous grains (barley starch, wheat starch, etc.)

✓ Vegetable gum (if made from wheat or oats)

✓ Frozen entrees, boxed meals, and canned meals

✓ Lunch meats, hot dogs, and other processed meats

✓ Vital wheat gluten

✓ Autolyzed or hydrolyzed yeast extract

SOURCES OF DAIRY

- ✓ Anything made with cream, butter, milk, yogurt, sour cream, or cheese
- ✓ Butter flavoring
- ✓ Whey protein
- ✓ Frozen entrees, boxed meals, and canned meals
- ✓ Salad dressings and condiments
- ✓ Whipped toppings
- ✓ Cake and frosting mixes

SOURCES OF REFINED SUGAR

- ✓ Anything made with granulated cane sugar, evaporated cane juice (or syrup), brown sugar, demerara sugar, golden sugar, turbinado sugar, confectioner's (powdered) sugar, maltose, maltodextrin, corn syrup, or high fructose corn syrup
- ✓ Breads, cereals, crackers, and cake and frosting mixes
- ✓ Canned tomato products and sauce
- ✓ Canned fruit
- ✓ Salad dressings
- ✓ Sauces and condiments (including nut butters)
- ✓ Soy sauce
- ✓ Ice cream and frozen desserts
- ✓ Frozen entrees, boxed meals, and canned meals
- ✓ Yogurt and other dairy products
- ✓ Some frozen fruits and vegetables

Other tips to keep in mind when you're shopping and reading labels:

1. Focus on the *ingredient* label, not the nutrition facts. You want to dig deeper than just the number of calories in the serving size of the product.

2. Look for hydrogenated and partially hydrogenated oils in the ingredient label, as these are trans-fats. Avoid them at all costs!

3. Don't be swayed by catchphrases. We've all seen them: *Low Fat! High Fiber! No Added Sugar! Made with Organic Ingredients!* Never buy a product based on a catchphrase. Always scour the label for the ingredients.

4. Take a look at the sodium and fiber content of the product. I'm often shocked at how much salt there is in something like organic sausages or how little fiber exists in that box of 100% whole grain cereal.

5. Shop the perimeter of the store. This is your best bet, because most foods around the perimeter of the store don't have labels to begin with! Focus on lean proteins, fruits, vegetables, grains and nuts from the bulk bins, and a few select products from the aisles. You'll bypass all of the labels and pare down your diet to the purest of foods.

6. Keep your receipts. You might get home and realize you just bought a product with gluten or sugar in it. Most grocery stores require a receipt for all unopened returned items, so make sure to save yours.

7. Go slow. When you begin shopping for pure foods, it takes time to "get into the groove," find your favorite brands, and so on. Give yourself plenty of time when shopping to allow for meticulous label-reading.

Remember that transitioning to a pure diet can be both exciting and greatly overwhelming at the same time. Try not to get caught up in all the little details or they will drag you down. Commit to one or two changes at a time. When those become easy, add a few more. This way you will ease into pure, decluttered living gradually and at your own pace, making the changes more sustainable in the long run. 🖋

Stocking the Pure Kitchen

Crucial to the success of adopting a pure lifestyle is stocking a pure kitchen. We all know that when the refrigerator is bare or the pantry shelves are empty, we're far more likely to make poor food choices than when the kitchen is laden with wholesome ingredients.

On the pages that follow are what I consider to be my pure living essentials. With a well-stocked kitchen, you'll find that it's easy and convenient to prepare nutritious meals and snacks. Before you fortify your kitchen with pure food, you'll need to purify it of unhealthy or old ingredients. Go through your kitchen shelf by shelf and cupboard by cupboard using the information in the previous chapters to guide the purging process.

For recommended brands and sources of specialty ingredients and equipment, see pages 225-226 of the Resources section.

In the Refrigerator & Freezer

Fruit: Keeping fresh fruit on hand makes a quick and healthy snack just an arm's length away. I always stock berries in my freezer as well for adding to smoothies, hot cereal, and baked goods.

✐ **Ginger root:** Fresh ginger root is not only packed with health-promoting, anti-inflammatory properties, but it also adds delicious zing to smoothies, marinades, soups, and more. Peel up the entire root of ginger when you get it home. Then place it in a plastic food storage bag and keep it in the freezer for several months. (It will wither up within a few days in the refrigerator.)

✐ **Herbs:** Flat-leaf parsley is my go-to herb whenever I need a pop of fresh flavor or a bright garnish for a dish. Cilantro, basil, dill, thyme, rosemary, and mint also add loads of flavor without salt, calories, or fat. Store herbs in a plastic bag with a damp paper towel wrapped around the stems.

✐ **Non-dairy milks:** You can make nut milk yourself by pureeing soaked nuts with water in a blender and then straining the liquids from the pulp. To save time, purchase unsweetened almond or rice milk at the grocery store. Keep it chilled for up to 10 days after opening.

✐ **Nuts, seeds, & nut butters:** Remember that nuts have oils and oils spoil. To keep nuts and seeds from going rancid, store them and butters made from them in the refrigerator or freezer. Walnuts, almonds, cashews, sunflower seeds, pumpkin seeds (pepitas), sesame seeds, ground flaxseed and chia seeds, and almond butter are my mainstays.

✐ **Proteins:** Lunches and dinners come together quickly if you have protein around to add some bulk to the meal. I usually cook up organic chicken breasts or thighs every week for salads and keep extra beef, fish, or poultry on hand either in the refrigerator if I'm using it right away or in the freezer for long-term storage.

✐ **Vegetables**: Devote a good chunk of your refrigerator and freezer real estate to colorful vegetables. Depending on the season, load up on whatever is fresh and at its peak. Store cut up vegetables such as carrots, celery, broccoli and cauliflower florets, and bell peppers

in airtight containers to have on hand for snacking or throwing into soups and stir-fries.

In the Pantry

Applesauce, unsweetened: **Applesauce, unsweetened:** Keep applesauce around for adding to baked goods and smoothies or enjoying as a healthy snack with nuts and cinnamon.

Baking soda & baking powder: Read labels to ensure that the product is manufactured in a way that avoids gluten cross-contamination.

Beans, canned: If you have time to cook your own beans from scratch, more power to you! But in a pinch, no-salt-added canned beans are a convenient substitute and primarily what I use.

Chicken & vegetable broth: Making your own broth is as easy as simmering a pot of water with organic chicken bones or vegetables for several hours, then seasoning it to taste. But when that's not an option, purchase low-sodium organic broths at the store to keep in your pantry.

Coconut milk, canned: For those eating dairy-free, coconut milk is a life saver! Keep a few cans (both light and full fat varieties) stocked in your pantry.

Dried fruit: Dried apricots, figs, dates, raisins, currants, and more kick a sweet tooth in a flash. They also act as natural sweeteners for baked goods and desserts.

Gluten-free pasta: Look for 100% brown rice or quinoa pasta, as some brands add starch or white rice flour to the noodles. (For my favorite brand, see page 226 of the Resources section.)

❧ **Lentils:** Because red, green, and brown lentils cook much more quickly than beans, it's easy to cook them from scratch. Always rinse your lentils before cooking them.

❧ **Spices:** A well-stocked spice drawer is the gateway to creative, flavorful meals with both variety and ethnic diversity. Anything goes, so experiment and find your favorites. Be on the lookout for anti-caking agents and other preservatives in many spices, as these are often hidden sources of gluten.

❧ **Tomatoes, canned:** If you have the time to can your own tomatoes in the summer, you deserve a pat on the back! When fresh tomatoes aren't available and if you don't can your own, organic canned tomatoes are great for throwing in soups, casseroles, sauces, and slow cooker meals.

❧ **Whole grains:** Brown rice, millet, and quinoa are inexpensive and highly nutritious. Rinsing quinoa before cooking helps to remove the bitter coating that the grain can sometimes have. Store your grains in airtight containers at room temperature. If you purchase them from the grocery store's bulk bins, be sure that the store has a quick turn-over rate to ensure freshness.

❧ **Vanilla extract:** It is generally accepted that vanilla extract is gluten-free, but it's not always sugar-free and comes in both alcohol and non-alcoholic varieties. Experiment with different vanilla extracts to find the one you like best, choosing organic if possible.

❧ **Vinegars:** I keep raw apple cider vinegar, red wine vinegar, balsamic vinegar, and brown rice vinegar in my pantry for a variety of uses including salad dressings, marinades, baked goods, and more.

Sweeteners

Agave nectar: Low-glycemic agave nectar is a syrup made from the agave plant with a consistency that's slightly thinner than honey. While agave is neutral in flavor, it is nearly twice as sweet as table sugar, allowing you to use less. I use certified organic dark amber agave nectar in my recipes.

Blackstrap molasses: When cane sugar is refined, the leftover product is molasses. Packed with iron and other minerals, molasses contributes a robust flavor to baked goods even when used in small amounts. Choose molasses labeled "unsulphured," as this means that no sulphur was used during the extraction process.

Coconut sugar: Also known as palm sugar, this unrefined granulated sweetener is low-glycemic and rich in vitamins and minerals. Coconut sugar is made from the sap of palm tree blossoms. With subtle molasses notes, coconut sugar is a less-moist and healthier alternative to brown sugar.

Honey: Honeys vary widely in flavor, color, and texture depending on the source of the nectar that the bees collected, making it a truly artisanal ingredient. Experiment with different varieties (alfalfa, clover, wildflower, and more) and find your favorite. I usually use organic clover honey in my baking for its mild flavor.

Maple syrup: More full-bodied and flavorful than agave nectar, maple syrup contains minerals including manganese and zinc. Grade A maple syrup is lighter in color and more refined than darker, nutrient-rich Grade B. Use the darkest, least refined kind of maple syrup you can find, preferably Grade B if it is available.

Gluten-Free Flours

In order to achieve ideal texture and flavor when baking gluten-free, you must use a blend of flours. There are dozens of gluten-free flour blends on the market that, while convenient, often consist of mostly starches, white rice flour, or corn flour. For optimal nutritional content, fiber, and flavor, I prefer to blend my own flours in varying combinations for different recipes.

Unless indicated below, you can store most gluten-free flours at room temperature. If your kitchen is particularly warm or you don't go through your flours very quickly, keep them refrigerated.

- **Blanched almond flour:** Made from finely ground blanched almonds, this high-protein, low-carbohydrate flour lends a lovely crumb to baked goods and does not taste gritty. Store almond flour in the refrigerator or freezer for up to six months to prevent it from going rancid. Note that almond flour is often labeled "almond meal."

- **Arrowroot starch:** Also called arrowroot powder or arrowroot flour, this ingredient is made from the ground roots of the arrowroot plant. It is an excellent thickener for pie fillings, sauces, and soups and gives gluten-free baked goods structure without strong flavor.

- **Brown rice flour:** Always use brown rice flour in conjunction with other flours when baking, as it often lends a gritty texture to the final product when used exclusively.

- **Buckwheat flour:** Perhaps my favorite gluten-free flour, recipes made with buckwheat flour pack hearty and earthy flavor into every bite. It pairs especially well with pumpkin and herbs.

- **Coconut flour:** I've nicknamed high-protein, high-fiber coconut flour "the sponge flour," because it has incredible liquid-soaking power! Contrary to what you might think, recipes made with coconut flour do not have a strong coconut flavor.

Cornmeal: Look for certified gluten-free cornmeal to avoid cross-contamination.

Millet flour: Millet is a hypoallergenic grain and a great one to introduce to young children when they begin eating solid food. Millet flour is made simply from ground millet and lends neutral color and flavor to whatever you use it in.

Sorghum flour: This flour works well as the base flour in just about any gluten-free baked good recipe. It is also relatively high in protein and fiber.

Tapioca starch: Also known as tapioca flour, this starch provides structure and some binding power to batters. It is milder in flavor than arrowroot starch, but the two can usually be used interchangeably.

Teff flour: Dark and hearty, teff flour is ground from tiny teff grains that are packed with iron, protein, and fiber. It pairs well with richly spiced recipes, chocolate or cocoa powder, and fruit and vegetable purees.

Unsweetened cocoa powder: Try both Dutch-processed and natural processed cocoa powder to determine which one you like better. I've used both interchangeably in most of my recipes and notice only slight variations in flavor. Use whichever one appeals to your palate.

Fats & Oils

Extra-virgin olive oil: A staple of the Mediterranean diet, extra-virgin olive oil is made from the first cold press of olives and is rich in heart-healthy fats. This oil is my go-to choice for most of my savory recipes. Purchase olive oil in dark glass bottles and store in a cool, dark place for no more than a few months.

✎ **Grapeseed oil:** This oil's smooth consistency and mild flavor lends well to baking. Purchase grapeseed oil in dark glass bottles and store in a cool, dark place for no more than a few months.

✎ **Virgin coconut oil:** Unrefined, organic, virgin coconut oil is a nutrient-packed saturated fat that may increase metabolism, aid in weight loss, improve skin tone, and fight bacteria. I find the flavor of coconut oil to be fairly neutral, although it may taste nutty or "tropical" to some palates. It works wonders as a substitute for butter in many recipes.

Essential Equipment & Tools

I'm not much of a gadget girl when it comes to cooking, but investing in a few good pieces of equipment and handy tools will make the process more enjoyable and yield better results.

✎ **Baking sheets:** Use rimmed baking sheets made of heavy stainless steel so they don't warp in the heat of the oven.

✎ **Blender:** Investing in my high-powered Vita-Mix blender was the best money I ever spent! A workhorse of a machine, my blender gets daily use for everything from green smoothies to cashew frostings. It runs as efficiently as the day I bought it.

✎ **Cake pans:** I have two standard 8-inch round cake pans, as this is the standard size called for in most recipes. I also keep a 9-inch spring-form pan on hand.

✎ **Colander & steamer basket:** Use a colander for draining pasta and canned beans and washing produce. A steamer basket is an inexpensive tool that makes it easy to steam vegetables without using a microwave.

✎ **Cutting boards:** My large wooden cutting board gets the most use of any of my kitchen tools. I also keep plastic boards on hand for cutting raw poultry, meat, and seafood.

Digital kitchen scale: I can't imagine life without my digital scale! It gets a daily workout weighing flours, tomatoes, potatoes, pasta, and more.

Dutch oven: Essentially just a heavy-bottomed pot, an enameled cast iron Dutch oven is useful for making soups, stews, roasted meats, and more. It can go from the stovetop to the oven safely and washes up very well.

Electric mixer: One year I was lucky enough to receive a KitchenAid stand mixer in ruby red as a birthday present. I'll admit that while I don't love it quite as much as my Vita-Mix, it makes whipping up batters a breeze. An electric handheld mixer will work well, too.

Food processor: From shredding vegetables to making baked goods to pureeing fruits, I use my food processor almost every day.

Immersion blender: A handheld immersion blender makes quick work of pureeing soups and sauces right in the pot so you don't have to deal with the fussy transfer of hot liquids to a blender or food processor.

Knives: If you only invest in one kitchen tool, let it be a good quality chef's knife. When you eat pure foods, you do *a lot* of chopping! Having sharp, heavy knifes that sit comfortably in your hand makes all the difference. Note that good quality knives are not necessarily the most expensive.

Measuring cups & spoons: Every cook needs a set or two of measuring utensils. Use stainless steel and glass so that hot liquids don't melt the plastic.

Microplane graters: These handheld graters are essential for grating citrus zest, nutmeg, fresh ginger, coconut, chocolate, and more. They are relatively inexpensive and hold their sharpness for a long time.

Mixing bowls: An assortment of stainless and glass mixing bowls gives you the freedom to make several recipes at once without having to wash bowls all the time.

Muffin pan: Having a muffin pan makes it easy to whip up a batch of homemade baked goods on the spur of the moment, as most muffin recipes don't take more than an hour from start to finish.

Parchment paper: Lining your baking sheets and pans with parchment paper eliminates the need for cooking spray and prolongs the life of your equipment. Use unbleached parchment if you can find it.

Pie dishes: Honestly, I don't make pie very often, but handcrafted ceramic pie plates are just too pretty to pass up! Most often I use mine as a baking dish for roasting chicken breasts or salmon.

Pizza cutter: I use my pizza cutter for slicing everything *but* pizza. It works well for scoring crackers and cutting biscuit dough.

Rolling pin: A heavy wooden rolling pin makes it easy to roll out dough with little effort.

Ruler: Keep a ruler in your utensil drawer and conveniently reach for it when a recipe calls for specific measurements (such as the thickness or diameter of dough).

Skillets, pots, & pans: Stainless steel cookware cleans up beautifully and lasts for decades. On a regular basis, I use a 12-inch skillet, 12-inch sauté pan, 6-inch fry pan, and three pots of varying sizes.

Slow cooker: For busy days when you just don't have time to cook, slow cookers have got your back. Throw some ingredients into the crock, leave the house for the day, and come home to a hot and healthy meal. I purchased my slow cooker for $20 or $30 at a hardware store and it works perfectly.

Ø **Storage containers:** Use glass storage containers with lids for leftovers. Glass jars also work well for storing ingredients like ground flaxseed, coconut milk, and dressings. Using glass over plastic eliminates the possibility of something with a dark pigment, such as curry powder or tomato sauce, to stain the container.

Ø **Utensils:** Every good cook needs their share of whisks, wooden spoons, rubber spatulas, and the all important tasting spoons. Silicone basting brushes and stainless steel tongs are also helpful tools.

THE RECIPES

. . . . .

Energizing Breakfasts

Breakfast. It's my favorite meal and one that I never skip. With nourishing food in my belly, I can start my day with energy, stamina, and focus. If you want to give your metabolism a kick-start and leap into the day full speed ahead, a healthy breakfast is a must.

Eating a homemade breakfast of *real foods* is a big step in the right direction toward adopting a pure lifestyle. Leave sugary cereals, yogurts, and pastries in the dust. The perfect breakfast blends complex carbohydrates with protein and fat for satiety. That may be a bowl of quinoa porridge topped with nuts and seeds or a fruit smoothie with flaxseed and protein powder. Eggs offer an excellent source of complete vegetarian protein in addition to B vitamins and vitamin A.

For children, a balanced breakfast is essential to optimal health. After a night without food, they literally need to "break the fast" and fuel their growing bodies with healthy carbohydrates, proteins, and fats. In this chapter, you'll find over a dozen recipes to please both kids and adults alike. From sweet mango rice porridge to whole grain pancakes to refreshing and creamy smoothies, you're guaranteed to find a breakfast that will kick your day off with an energized bang.

Green "Creamsicle" Smoothie

Serves 1 — **Vegan**

I love this quote from Dr. Mark Hyman: "The fork is your most powerful tool to change your health and the planet; food is the most powerful medicine to heal chronic illness." Health starts in our homes, in our kitchens. It's what we eat that makes us who we are. This smoothie is a favorite mine that makes for a healing breakfast or snack. It's nutrient-packed but you'd never know it from the luscious taste.

½ **medium ripe banana**

½ **cup frozen mango or pineapple chunks**

1 cup mild greens, such as baby spinach or mache

1 (2-inch) piece cucumber, peeled

¼ **medium ripe avocado**

¼ **cup unsweetened almond milk**

¼ **cup water**

Combine all of the ingredients in a blender and blend on high until smooth. Serve.

....

Go Nut-free: Use rice milk instead of the almond milk.

....

Turn-Back-the-Clock Smoothie

Serves 1 — **Vegan**

This invigorating smoothie has age-reversing superpowers! Antioxidant-packed blueberries deliver loads of cancer-fighting compounds, while the chia seeds provide essential fatty acids to give skin a healthy glow. The orange zest and cinnamon lace the smoothie with refreshing "zing" to balance out the sweetness from the banana. For extra kick, add ¼ teaspoon of finely grated fresh ginger root.

½ cup frozen blueberries

½ medium ripe banana

½ cup unsweetened almond milk, rice milk, or water

1 scoop brown rice, pea, or hemp protein powder (optional)

2 teaspoons ground chia seeds

½ teaspoon finely grated orange zest

¼ teaspoon ground cinnamon

Combine all of the ingredients in a blender and blend on high until smooth. Serve.

Technique Tip: If you have a Vita-Mix or other high-powered blender, there's no need to grate the orange zest. Just throw in a strip of the peel and the machine will do the work for you.

Cherry Ginger Smoothie

Serves 1 — **Vegan, nut-free**

This anti-inflammatory smoothie is packed with pain-killing power. Cherries get their vibrant red color from flavanoid molecules that exert a vast array of beneficial effects on the body, including the production of anti-inflammatory enzymes that have been shown to significantly reduce pain. Ginger also contains potent compounds called gingerols that may reduce arthritis pain and improve joint mobility when consumed regularly. So the next time you're feeling a little achy, gulp down a glass of this smoothie and do your body a world of good.

½ cup frozen cherries

½ medium ripe pear, peeled and chopped

¼ medium ripe avocado

½ cup water

1 teaspoon finely grated ginger root

Pinch of ground cinnamon

Combine all of the ingredients in a blender and blend on high until smooth and creamy. Serve.

> **Ingredient Tip:** If your pears are rock hard when you bring them home from the store, place them on the kitchen counter in a paper bag for a day or two to ripen them more quickly. To speed up the process even more, add an apple or banana to the bag.

Pure Power Smoothie

Serves 1 — **Vegan**

Brimming with antioxidants from the fruit, satiating fats from the seeds and nut butter, muscle-building protein from the powder, and blood sugar-balancing cinnamon, nothing kicks my day off to a better start than a tall glass of this smoothie. When shopping for a protein powder, be on guard for hidden sources of gluten, dairy, and sugar that often sneak into the ingredient lists.

½ cup fresh strawberries or blueberries

½ medium frozen banana

2 ice cubes

½ cup unsweetened almond or rice milk

1 scoop brown rice, pea, or hemp protein powder

2 teaspoons ground chia seeds or flaxseed

1 tablespoon almond or peanut butter

Pinch of sea salt

Pinch of ground cinnamon

Combine all of the ingredients in a blender and blend on high until smooth. Serve.

Go Nut-free: Use rice milk and omit the nut butter.

Chow down to stay thin.

Studies have shown that people who eat breakfast
are more likely to be an ideal weight than those who do not.
Eating first thing in the morning kick-starts your metabolism
and keeps your engine burning all day long.

Herb & Heirloom Tomato Frittata

*Serves 4 — **Nut-free***

Frittatas top my list of favorite brunch dishes to serve to guests. Easy to make but still impressive, I like to pair this one with a tossed green salad, oven-roasted potatoes, and the Cinnamon Currant Biscuits on page 90. If you can't find heirloom tomatoes, regular or Roma tomatoes are a fine substitute.

8 large eggs

2 tablespoons finely chopped flat-leaf parsley

2 tablespoons snipped or finely chopped chives

½ teaspoon sea salt

2 tablespoons extra-virgin olive oil

½ medium yellow onion, finely chopped

2 garlic cloves, finely chopped

½ pound heirloom tomatoes (any variety and color), thinly sliced

¼ cup thinly sliced fresh basil

Preheat the oven to 400°F. In a large bowl, whisk together the eggs, parsley, chives, and salt. Set aside.

Heat the olive oil in a 10- to 12-inch skillet over medium heat. Add the onion and cook until soft and translucent, about 5 minutes. Add the garlic and stir for 1 minute. Add the herbed egg mixture and cook undisturbed for 1-2 minutes until barely set around the edges. While the eggs cook, scatter the tomatoes over the top.

Transfer the skillet to the oven and bake for about 12 minutes until the frittata is puffed and golden. Sprinkle with the basil, cut into wedges, and serve.

....

Egg-cellent Eggs

Often touted as nature's perfect protein, eggs are a powerhouse worthy of inclusion beyond just breakfast. A good source of vitamin B12 as well as a variety of minerals, they offer loads of nutrition with few calories, making them an all-star choice for those watching their weight.

....

Huevos Rancheros Quesadillas

Serves 4

A breakfast like this one is guaranteed to stick with you. It's also one of my favorite dinners. Here I've turned huevos rancheros, a traditional Mexican dish consisting of eggs and black beans served up with corn or flour tortillas, into good old eat-them-with-your-hands quesadillas. The mashed beans and salsa create a tasty "glue" that holds them together, eliminating the need for cheese.

1 tablespoon virgin coconut oil

¼ cup finely chopped red onion

4 large eggs

1 tablespoon finely chopped cilantro or flat-leaf parsley

¼ teaspoon sea salt

1 cup cooked black beans

¼ cup salsa (plus more for serving)

½ teaspoon chili powder

¼ teaspoon ground cumin

8 (6-inch) gluten-free corn tortillas

1 medium ripe avocado, halved, pitted, and thinly sliced

1 tablespoon extra-virgin olive oil

Heat the coconut oil in a large skillet over medium heat. Add the onion and cook, stirring often, until soft and translucent, about 2 minutes. While the onion cooks, whisk together the eggs, parsley, and sea salt. Add the egg mixture to the sautéed onions and cook, stirring frequently with a rubber spatula, until the eggs are scrambled and set but still moist, about 2 minutes. Remove from heat and set aside.

In a medium bowl, mash the beans, ¼ cup salsa, chili powder, and cumin with a fork. Arrange the tortillas in an even layer on a work surface and spread each with an equal amount of the black bean mash. Divide the scrambled eggs among 4 of the tortillas and top with the avocado slices. Place the remaining 4 tortillas, bean side down, on top of the tortillas with the eggs to create quesadillas.

Heat the olive oil over medium heat in a very large skillet. Add 2 of the quesadillas and cook for 2-3 minutes per side, flipping with care. Remove from the pan. (Transfer to a warm oven if desired to keep the quesadillas hot.) Add the remaining 2 quesadillas and repeat the cooking process.

Cut each quesadilla in half and serve with additional salsa.

Spanish-Style
Baked Eggs over Rice

Serves 4 — **Nut-free**

Breakfast for dinner is one of my go-to meals when I don't know what else to make. This dish is easy but elegant, making it perfect for breakfast, brunch, or—my personal favorite—dinner.

1 cup long grain brown rice

2 cups water

1 tablespoon extra-virgin olive oil

½ medium red onion, chopped

1 small red bell pepper, seeded and chopped

4 cloves garlic, finely chopped

1 teaspoon dried oregano

¼ teaspoon crushed red pepper flakes

**1 (14-ounce) can artichoke hearts (packed in water),
     drained and roughly chopped**

1 (28-ounce) can diced tomatoes, preferably fire-roasted

½ cup water

Sea salt and black pepper, to taste

8 large eggs

¼ cup finely chopped flat-leaf parsley

Bring the rice and water to a boil in a medium pot over high heat. Reduce the heat to low, cover, and simmer until the water is absorbed and the rice is fluffy, 35-45 minutes. Let the rice stand off heat, covered, on the stove until ready to serve.

Preheat the oven to 400°F. Heat the olive oil in a large saucepan over medium-high heat. Add the onion and bell pepper. Cook, stirring occasionally, for about 5 minutes. Add the garlic, oregano, and red pepper flakes. Stir for 1 minute. Add the artichoke hearts and diced tomatoes. Bring the sauce to a boil, then reduce the heat to medium-low and simmer for 10-15 minutes to blend the flavors. Season the sauce to taste with salt and pepper.

Transfer the sauce to a 9x13-inch glass baking dish. Create 8 indentations in the sauce with the back of a spoon and crack an egg into each indentation. Bake until the eggs are just set, about 20 minutes. Sprinkle with the parsley. Serve the eggs and sauce over the rice.

Make-ahead Tip: Make the tomato and artichoke sauce up to 1 day in advance. Keep refrigerated in an airtight container until ready to use.

Potato & Vegetable Hash
with Eggs Any Style

Serves 4 — **Nut-free**

Want a recipe that you can't mess up, even if you try? This is it! I love hash for its ease of preparation and the way it turns out a little differently every time. Change it up with whatever seasonal vegetables you have on hand, or try the curried cauliflower variation below. Apart from being a hearty and satisfying way to start the day, hash also makes an easy side dish for grilled chicken, steak, or fish.

1 pound red potatoes, washed and cut into ½-inch chunks

2 tablespoons extra-virgin olive oil

1 medium yellow onion, chopped

1 medium red bell pepper, seeded and chopped

3 cups bite-sized broccoli florets

1 teaspoon ground cumin

3 garlic cloves, finely chopped

1 cup frozen peas, thawed

¼ cup finely chopped flat-leaf parsley

Sea salt and black pepper, to taste

8 large eggs, cooked any style you like them

OPTIONAL TOPPINGS:

Diced avocado

Chopped tomatoes or salsa

Sprouts

Place the potatoes in a medium pot and cover with cold water. Bring to a boil over high heat. Reduce the heat to medium and continue to boil the potatoes until just barely tender to the bite, 8-10 minutes. Drain and set aside.

Heat the olive oil in a large sauté pan or Dutch oven over medium-high heat. Add the onion, bell pepper, and broccoli. Cook, stirring occasionally, until the onion is soft and translucent, about 5 minutes. Reduce the heat to medium and add the reserved potatoes. Cook, stirring occasionally, until the potatoes are light brown in spots, 5-8 minutes.

Add the cumin and garlic. Stir for 1 minute. Add the peas and parsley. Cook for 2-3 minutes to heat through. Season to taste with salt and lots of black pepper.

Serve the hash with the cooked eggs and top as desired.

Curried Potato & Cauliflower Hash:

Swap in bite-sized cauliflower florets for the broccoli and replace the cumin with 2 teaspoons of curry powder.

Flourless Banana-Nut Breakfast Cookies

Makes about 20 cookies — **Vegan**

Sweetened entirely with fruit, these flourless cookies make a delicious grab-and-go breakfast or satisfying afternoon snack. Soft and moist, they rely on quinoa flakes rather than flour for their structure. Quinoa flakes, essentially just steam-rolled quinoa, can be found in the bulk foods section of your natural foods store or in the hot cereal aisle.

1 cup (packed) pitted Medjool dates

2 cups quinoa flakes

⅔ cup (64 grams) blanched almond flour

1 teaspoon ground cinnamon

½ teaspoon baking soda

½ teaspoon sea salt

3 medium very ripe bananas, peeled and broken into chunks

2 tablespoons virgin coconut oil, room temperature

1 teaspoon vanilla extract

½ cup chopped pecans

Preheat the oven to 350°F. Line 2 baking sheets with parchment paper. Cover the dates with hot water in a small bowl and soak for 10 minutes.

While the dates soak, whisk together the quinoa flakes, almond flour, cinnamon, baking soda, and salt in a large mixing bowl.

Drain the dates, reserving 1 tablespoon of the soaking liquid. Place the dates and reserved liquid into the bowl of a food processor fitted with the steel blade. Add the bananas, coconut oil, and vanilla. Process until the mixture is smooth and the dates are reduced to small flecks, about 1 minute. Pour the banana mixture into the dry ingredients. Stir with a wooden spoon to combine. Stir in the pecans.

Drop heaping tablespoons of the dough onto the parchment-lined baking sheets. Flatten each cookie to ½-inch thick using the back of a spoon or your fingertips.

Bake the cookies for about 12 minutes or until lightly browned and firm to the touch. Cool completely on the baking sheets before serving or storing. Store in an airtight container in the refrigerator.

....

Delectable Dates

If you think you don't like dates, you still might
want to try them in baked goods and desserts.
Once pureed and incorporated with other ingredients,
dates lend natural sweetness without overpowering
the recipe with date flavor.

....

Grain-Free Granola Balls

Makes 15-20 balls — **Egg-free**

By far one of the most popular recipes on my blog, these balls of "mock granola" are addictive. Really. I dare you to stop at just one.

½ cup raw sunflower seeds

½ cup raw pumpkin seeds

½ cup (48 grams) blanched almond flour

1 teaspoon ground cinnamon

½ teaspoon sea salt

1 cup raw walnuts, chopped

¼ cup dried blueberries or currants

¼ cup raisins

¼ cup plus 1 tablespoon honey

2 tablespoons creamy almond butter

1 tablespoon water

½ teaspoon vanilla extract

Preheat the oven to 350°F. Line a baking sheet with parchment paper.

In a food processor fitted with the steel blade, combine the sunflower seeds, pumpkin seeds, almond flour, cinnamon, and salt. Pulse for ten 1-second pulses to form a coarse meal. Transfer to a medium mixing bowl.

Stir in the walnuts, blueberries, and raisins. Add the honey, almond butter, water, and vanilla. Stir to combine with a wooden spoon. The dough will be thick and stiff. Using slightly wet hands, form the dough into tightly packed balls about 1 inch in diameter. Arrange the balls 2 inches apart on the parchment-lined baking sheet.

Bake for 20-22 minutes until deeply golden brown. The balls will be soft to the touch. Cool completely before serving or storing. The balls will set up as they cool. Store in an airtight container.

....

Technique Tip: When forming the balls, keep a glass of water beside you. Then you can conveniently moisten your hands as needed to keep the dough from sticking.

....

Pumpkin Oatmeal Breakfast Clusters

Makes about 22 — **Vegan**

These clusters are like a bowl of oatmeal in portable, handheld form. Moist and chewy, they're a perfect quick breakfast or afternoon snack paired with a cup of herbal tea.

2 ½ cups gluten-free rolled oats

½ cup raisins

¼ cup chopped walnuts

¼ cup raw sunflower seeds

¼ cup ground flaxseed

2 teaspoons ground cinnamon

¼ teaspoon sea salt

½ cup canned pure pumpkin puree

1 medium ripe banana, mashed well

¼ cup unsweetened applesauce

¼ cup grapeseed oil

2 tablespoons dark maple syrup

Preheat the oven to 350°F. Line 2 baking sheets with parchment paper.

In a large mixing bowl, combine the oats, raisins, walnuts, sunflower seeds, flax-seed, cinnamon, and salt. In a separate bowl, whisk together the pumpkin puree, banana, applesauce, grapeseed oil, and maple syrup. Stir the wet ingredients into the dry until thoroughly incorporated.

Form the mixture into tightly-packed cookie shapes about ½-inch thick using a scant ¼-cup (packed) per cluster. Arrange the clusters at least 1 inch apart on the baking sheets. Bake for about 20 minutes or until lightly browned and firm to the touch. Cool completely and store in an airtight container.

Whole Grain
Applesauce Pancakes

Makes about 15 (3-4 inch) pancakes

Pancakes were one of my favorite breakfasts as a kid. After early morning romps in the snow with my sister, there was nothing more comforting then coming inside to a table laden with pancakes, maple syrup, and fresh fruit. Gluten-free and packed with fiber-rich whole grains and flaxseed, these pancakes are equally enjoyed (and gobbled down) by both kids and adults.

½ cup (65 grams) millet flour

½ cup (60 grams) buckwheat flour

½ cup (52 grams) tapioca starch

¼ cup ground flaxseed

1 tablespoon plus 1 teaspoon baking powder

1 teaspoon baking soda

1 teaspoon ground cinnamon

1 teaspoon sea salt

1 cup unsweetened applesauce

½ cup unsweetened almond or rice milk

¼ cup virgin coconut oil, melted and cooled (plus more for the pan)

2 large eggs

OPTIONAL TOPPINGS:

Sliced bananas, strawberries, pears, peaches, or other seasonal fruit

Fruit-sweetened jam

Dark maple syrup

Almond or cashew butter

Preheat the oven to 200°F. Set a wire rack on a baking sheet and put it in the oven.

In a large bowl, whisk together the flours, flaxseed, baking powder, baking soda, cinnamon, and salt. In a separate bowl, whisk together the applesauce, almond milk, melted coconut oil, and eggs. Stir the wet ingredients into the dry to combine.

Heat up a tablespoon or so of coconut oil in a large skillet over medium heat. When it has melted, drop the batter by ¼-cupful into the skillet and cook for 2-3 minutes. The batter will be thick, so you may need to use the back of the measuring cup to spread the pancakes out a bit. Flip the pancakes and continue to cook for another 2 minutes. Transfer the pancakes to the wire rack in the warm oven. Repeat the process until all of the batter is used, melting more coconut oil as needed in the skillet to prevent the pancakes from sticking.

Serve warm with desired toppings.

··

Tips for Perfect Pancakes

✓ Don't overcrowd the pancakes in your pan. I usually cook three or four at a time. Any more than that makes flipping them difficult.

✓ If your skillet accumulates little burnt crisps of batter as you cook the pancakes, wipe it out with a paper towel in between batches to keep it clean.

✓ After the first batch or two of pancakes, your skillet will be good and hot—maybe too hot. Start out working over medium heat, but keep in mind that you may need to lower the heat to medium-low as you continue cooking pancakes. (Consequently, as the skillet becomes hotter, your pancakes may cook quicker.)

··

Cream of Quinoa
with Cinnamon Berry Compote

*Serves 4 — **Vegan***

Quinoa, a good source of complete protein, cooks more quickly than rice or millet. You can make the compote in advance and reheat it before serving. It's also delicious over the Whole Grain Applesauce Pancakes on page 70.

1 ½ cups frozen blueberries

1 ½ cups frozen raspberries

2 tablespoons fresh orange juice

2 teaspoons finely grated orange zest

2 teaspoons ground cinnamon

3 tablespoons dark maple syrup, divided

1 ¼ cups quinoa, rinsed and drained

3 cups water, divided

¼ teaspoon sea salt

¾ cup canned coconut milk (full fat)

Chopped walnuts or pecans, for topping

In a small pot over medium-high heat, bring the blueberries, raspberries, orange juice and zest, cinnamon, and 1 tablespoon of the maple syrup to a rapid simmer. Cook, stirring often, for 4-5 minutes until the mixture is thick and syrupy. Set aside and cover to keep warm.

In a medium pot, bring the quinoa, 2 ½ cups water, and the salt to a boil over medium heat. Reduce the heat to low, cover, and simmer until the water is absorbed and the quinoa is fluffy, about 15 minutes. Add the remaining 2 tablespoons maple syrup, remaining ½ cup water, and the coconut milk. Increase the heat to medium and cook, stirring often, until the mixture is thick and porridge-like, 2-3 minutes.

Serve bowls of the quinoa topped with the berry compote and nuts.

Tropical Mango Rice Porridge

Serves 4 — **Vegan**

I fell in love with mangos and macadamia nuts on my first trip to Hawaii. Shopping at the local farmers' market several times a week presented me with many opportunities to savor the fresh foods harvested right from the islands. Now, whenever I eat a bowl of this porridge or enjoy a morning fruit bowl with mangos and macadamias, visions of swaying palm trees and sandy beaches cascade through my memory. This porridge offers me a little trip to the tropics without all the travel!

1 large or 2 small ripe mangos, peeled, seeded, and chopped (about 2 cups)

2 tablespoons dark maple syrup, or more to taste

1 cup short grain brown rice

2 cups water

¼ teaspoon ground ginger

¼ teaspoon ground cardamom

¼ teaspoon sea salt

½ cup canned coconut milk (full fat)

¼ cup water

Chopped macadamia nuts, for serving

In a food processor fitted with the steel blade, process the mangos with 2 tablespoons of the maple syrup until smooth. Transfer to a bowl and set aside.

In a medium pot over high heat, bring the rice, water, ginger, cardamom, and salt to a boil. Reduce the heat to low, cover, and simmer until the water is absorbed, 35-45 minutes.

When the rice is cooked, stir in the coconut milk and water. Simmer over low heat for about 2 minutes until the mixture is the consistency of thick porridge. Stir in the mango puree and bring back up to a simmer. Cook, stirring often, for 2-3 minutes to heat the puree through and thicken the porridge slightly. Taste and add more maple syrup if desired.

Serve bowls of the porridge topped with macadamia nuts.

Wholesome Baked Goods

True confession: I'm not the best baker in the bunch. As much as I love the process of measuring flour, whisking batter, and watching cakes and muffins rise to golden domes in the oven, I will never be an expert baker. I have more than my fair share of rock-hard muffin stories and crumbly cake disasters that I could tell you, believe me!

When I set out to write the baked good recipes for this book, I kept two criteria in mind. First, the recipes had to be easy enough for me—a novice gluten-free baker—to pull off. And second, they had to be somewhat healthy. No way was I about to spend a big chunk of my time in the kitchen on a recipe only to produce something that lacked good nutrition.

The recipes on the pages that follow (and those that are baked in the Sweets & Treats chapter on pages 195-221) made the cut. Not only are they relatively easy to throw together, but they also incorporate an array of healthy ingredients ranging from natural sweeteners to fruit purees to fiber-rich whole grains. And best of all? Every bite is packed with delicious, wholesome flavor.

Retraining Your Taste Buds

Approach the recipes in this chapter with an open mind and palate. You simply cannot expect a muffin with buckwheat flour, coconut oil, and maple syrup to taste like one made with wheat flour, butter, and white sugar. Learn to appreciate the flavors and textures of these recipes for what they are instead of comparing them to what you think they should be.

In my baking, I use natural sweeteners in place of refined sugar and use less than most typical recipes to lend subtle, "background sweetness" and let the other flavors in the recipe shine through. Training your taste buds to respond positively to less sweet baked goods will take time, but before you know it, you'll be shocked at how sweet something like a banana can taste after you've been avoiding refined sugar for a while.

A Bit of Advice for Gluten-Free Bakers

They say that cooking is an art and baking is a science. I believe that gluten-free baking requires a tasteful blend of both. Becoming both an artist and a scientist in the kitchen is no easy task. Having said that, remember that the best way to learn is by doing. The more you get in that kitchen and practice your skills as a baker, the more confident and improved you'll become.

Along the way, I guarantee that you'll have plenty of kitchen nightmares along with those long-awaited, hard-earned, triumphant successes. Through it all, remember to hold your chin up and keep on keeping on. Gluten-free baking is much like life. It has its ups and downs, but the height of those ups and depth of those downs hinge on one crucial variable: your attitude. It's up to you to make it a positive one! 🖋

10 Tips for Successful Baking

1. Read the recipe all the way through before starting. Preparation paves the way to success! By reading the entire recipe before jumping in, you'll know what to expect and can be better prepared and equipped.

2. Follow the recipe as it's written before making changes to it.

3. Invest in good quality pans and baking equipment. Think of them as your "tools of the trade." Remember that less than adequate equipment will produce less than adequate results.

4. Measure your flour properly. Here's how: stir up the flour in the container or bag before measuring. This incorporates air, often leading to lighter baked goods. Scoop the flour into the measuring cup using a spoon. Use a flat edge, such as a butter knife, to level the flour flush with the top of the cup. Do not pack the flour into the cup or use "rounded" cups. You will have more flour than you need, leading to various problems that may arise during baking.

5. Use that parchment paper! It's a baker's best friend as it prevents sticking and prolongs the life of your pans. If it's not heavily soiled, you can reuse it several times as well.

6. Do not open the oven door more than is necessary. Heat escapes from the oven every time you open the door, causing your baked goods to take longer to cook and leading to uneven heat distribution.

7. Begin checking on a recipe a few minutes before the recipe says it will be done. For example, if the recipe says to bake a pan of muffins for 15-18 minutes, begin checking on them at 13 or 14. Some ovens run hotter than others. Doing this will prevent over-baking or burning.

8. Unless otherwise instructed, cool your gluten-free baked goods completely before serving or storing them. Gluten gives baked goods structure and substance. Without it, your treats will have more of a tendency to crumble or break apart when handled. Cooling them significantly improves this problem, especially when it's something like a quick bread that has to be sliced.

9. Take your environment into consideration when storing your baked goods. If you live in a humid climate, chances are you'll want to eat them up right away or store them in the refrigerator or freezer instead of on the countertop. Gluten-free baked goods do not always maintain the same textural integrity over time as wheat baked goods do, so I find that most are best eaten on the day they are made for optimal flavor.

10. If the recipe doesn't turn out for you on the first take, don't give up. It may be the weather that day, an incorrect measurement of flour or another ingredient, or simply a fluke. Keep trying!

....

Bonus Tip: While not essential, I strongly encourage you to invest in a digital kitchen scale. Weighing your flours is the most accurate form of measurement. You'll note in these recipes that I provide the flour measurements in cups as well as grams. Using a scale to weigh your flours ensures that you're not overfilling or under-filling your cups. Also, if you want to swap one flour for another (say sorghum for brown rice), the weight of the flours varies, so you should substitute by weight instead of volume. I can tell you from firsthand experience that after purchasing and using a digital kitchen scale, you'll wonder how you ever lived without it!

....

Seeded Breakfast Muffins

Makes 12 — **Nut-free**

Buckwheat flour gives these muffins an earthy, full-bodied flavor that I just can't get enough of. Not too sweet on their own, the muffins pair perfectly with fruit spread or jam and make a healthful addition to school lunch boxes.

¾ cup (78 grams) sorghum flour

½ cup (60 grams) buckwheat flour

½ cup (52 grams) tapioca starch

2 tablespoons ground flaxseed

1 teaspoon ground cinnamon

1 teaspoon baking powder

1 teaspoon baking soda

¼ teaspoon sea salt

2 large eggs

⅓ cup grapeseed oil

⅓ cup dark maple syrup

⅓ cup unsweetened applesauce

1 medium Gala apple, peeled, cored, and chopped small

½ cup raisins

FOR TOPPING:

1 tablespoon raw sunflower seeds

1 tablespoon raw pumpkin seeds

1 tablespoon raw sesame seeds

Preheat the oven to 350°F. Line 12 cups of a standard muffin pan with paper liners.

In a large bowl, whisk together the sorghum flour, buckwheat flour, tapioca starch, flaxseed, cinnamon, baking powder, baking soda, and salt. In a separate bowl, whisk together the eggs, oil, maple syrup, and applesauce. Pour the wet ingredients into the dry and stir well to combine. Stir in the apple and raisins.

Divide the batter evenly among the lined muffin cups. Combine the seeds in a small bowl. Sprinkle the tops of the muffins with the seed mixture. Bake for 16-18 minutes until a toothpick inserted into a muffin comes out clean. Cool completely in the pan before serving. Store the muffins in an airtight container.

Spring Rhubarb Muffins

*Makes 12 — **Nut-free***

I make these muffins during a short window in the spring when rhubarb floods into my farmers' market. Not too sweet, the muffins showcase rhubarb's tart flavor beautifully without making your mouth pucker. The subtle hint of orange infuses even more fresh spring flavor into these gems.

¾ **cup (78 grams) sorghum flour**

½ **cup (67 grams) brown rice flour**

½ **cup (52 grams) tapioca starch**

2 tablespoons ground flaxseed

1 teaspoon baking powder

1 teaspoon baking soda

¼ **teaspoon sea salt**

2 large eggs

¼ **cup plus 2 tablespoons grapeseed oil**

¼ **cup plus 2 tablespoons agave nectar**

⅓ **cup fresh orange juice**

1 tablespoon finely grated orange zest

1 cup chopped rhubarb

Coconut sugar, for sprinkling (optional)

Preheat the oven to 350°F. Line 12 cups of a standard muffin pan with paper liners.

In a large bowl, whisk together the sorghum flour, brown rice flour, tapioca starch, flaxseed, baking powder, baking soda, and sea salt. In a separate bowl, whisk together the eggs, oil, agave nectar, orange juice, and orange zest. Pour the wet ingredients into the dry and stir well to combine. Stir in the rhubarb.

Divide the batter evenly among the lined muffin cups. Sprinkle the tops with a bit of coconut sugar, if using. Bake for 15-18 minutes until golden brown and a toothpick inserted into a muffin comes out clean. Cool completely in pan before serving. Store the muffins in an airtight container.

....

The Power of Citrus

The orange juice and zest in this recipe bring another
flavor dimension to the muffins and help to tame the tartness
of the rhubarb. Adding zest to your baked goods elevates
the "yum factor" and gives them an extra punch of both
flavor and fragrance.

....

Cranberry Oatmeal Muffins

Makes 12 muffins

Sweet but not cloying, durable but not dense, these muffins pack everything I love about healthy baking into just a few bites: whole grain goodness, a fancy flair from the orange zest and cranberries, and delicate sweetness from the dark maple syrup.

¾ cup unsweetened almond or rice milk

¼ cup plus 2 tablespoons virgin coconut oil

1 cup gluten-free rolled oats

½ cup dark maple syrup

1 teaspoon vanilla extract

¾ cup (78 grams) sorghum flour

⅓ cup (35 grams) tapioca starch

¼ cup (30 grams) buckwheat flour

1 tablespoon ground flaxseed

2 teaspoons baking powder

1 teaspoon ground cinnamon

½ teaspoon ground ginger

¼ teaspoon sea salt

2 large eggs

1 tablespoon finely grated orange zest

2/3 cup dried cranberries, preferably fruit juice sweetened

½ cup chopped walnuts (optional)

Preheat the oven to 350°F. Line 12 cups of a standard muffin pan with paper liners.

Bring the almond milk and coconut oil to a simmer in a small pot over medium heat. Remove from heat and transfer to a medium bowl. Stir in the oats, maple syrup, and vanilla extract and set aside to soak for 5-10 minutes.

In a large bowl, whisk together the sorghum flour, tapioca flour, buckwheat flour, flaxseed, baking powder, cinnamon, ginger, and salt. Add the eggs and orange zest to the oatmeal mixture and whisk to combine. Add the wet ingredients to the flour mixture and stir to combine. Fold in the dried cranberries and walnuts, if using.

Divide the batter evenly among the prepared muffin cups. Bake for 15-20 minutes until a toothpick inserted into the center of a muffin comes out clean. Cool completely before removing from pan. Store the muffins in an airtight container.

Apple Snack Cakes
with Oatmeal Topping

Makes 12

The light, luxurious texture of these cakes impresses me every time I make them. Delicate but sturdy, they make an indulgent afternoon snack with a cup of tea or the perfect little treat to tuck inside a lunch box.

FOR THE CAKES:

1 cup (96 grams) blanched almond flour

¾ cup (96 grams) millet flour

½ cup (54 grams) arrowroot starch

½ cup coconut sugar

2 teaspoons baking powder

1 teaspoon baking soda

1 teaspoon ground cinnamon

¼ teaspoon sea salt

3 large egg whites

**1 medium Gala apple, peeled and shredded on the large holes
    of a box grater**

¼ cup plus 1 tablespoon grapeseed oil

FOR THE OATMEAL TOPPING:

½ cup gluten-free rolled oats

2 tablespoons (16 grams) millet flour

2 tablespoons coconut sugar

2 tablespoons extra-virgin olive oil

1 tablespoon dark maple syrup

Preheat the oven to 350°F. Line 12 cups of a standard muffin pan with paper liners.

In a large bowl, whisk together the almond flour, millet flour, arrowroot starch, coconut sugar, baking powder, baking soda, cinnamon, and sea salt. In a separate bowl, vigorously whisk the egg whites until they are foamy. Whisk in the grated apple and grapeseed oil. Using a rubber spatula, stir the wet ingredients into the dry until combined. Divide the batter evenly among the lined muffin cups.

In a small bowl, mix together the ingredients for the topping. Sprinkle the topping evenly over the cakes. Bake for 18-20 minutes until golden brown and a toothpick inserted into the center of a cake comes out clean.

Cool cakes completely in the pan before serving. Store in an airtight container.

Variation: Add 1 tablespoon of finely grated orange zest to the wet ingredients for a hint of citrus flavor.

Zucchini Bread
with Dried Cherries

Makes one 9x5-inch loaf

Moist and tender, you'd never know that this bread was gluten-free. Just make sure to cool the loaf completely before slicing to ensure durable slices.

½ cup (48 grams) blanched almond flour

½ cup (52 grams) sorghum flour

½ cup (54 grams) arrowroot starch

¼ cup (30 grams) buckwheat flour

2 tablespoons ground flaxseed

2 teaspoons baking powder

1 teaspoon baking soda

¼ teaspoon sea salt

½ cup coconut sugar

1 cup (packed) coarsely grated zucchini (about 1 medium zucchini)

⅓ cup extra-virgin olive oil

¼ cup unsweetened almond or rice milk

1 large egg plus 1 large egg white, lightly beaten

1 teaspoon apple cider vinegar

½ cup dried cherries, preferably fruit juice sweetened

Preheat the oven to 350°F. Line a 9x5-inch loaf pan with parchment paper, leaving a 2-inch overhang on all sides.

In a medium bowl, whisk together the almond flour, sorghum flour, arrowroot starch, buckwheat flour, flaxseed, baking powder, baking soda, sea salt, and coconut sugar.

Place the grated zucchini in a clean kitchen towel and squeeze it dry of as much liquid as possible. In a medium bowl, whisk the zucchini with the olive oil, almond milk, egg and egg white, and vinegar. Pour the zucchini mixture into the dry ingredients and stir to combine. Fold in the dried cherries.

Pour the batter into the parchment-lined loaf pan. Bake for about 40 minutes or until a knife inserted into the center of the loaf comes out clean. Cool the bread completely in the pan before removing and slicing with a serrated knife. Store the bread tightly wrapped in an airtight container.

....

Technique Tip: Leaving an overhang of parchment
paper when you line the pan makes for quick and easy
removal once the loaf is cool.

....

Teff Banana Bread

Makes one 9x5-inch loaf

This loaf comes out just as moist and beautiful as the banana bread you're probably used to, but because it relies mostly on the bananas for sweetness, it will not taste as sweet as a traditional loaf. The teff flour adds texture, body, and flavor to the bread while the bananas lend moisture and a delicate layer of fruitiness. I encourage you to make this bread at least once just as you see it below before adding more sweetener. If you'd prefer a sweeter bread, increase the coconut sugar to ½ cup or more. I enjoy the less sweet version spread with a little honey or jam.

½ cup (68 grams) teff flour

½ cup (54 grams) arrowroot starch

½ cup (48 grams) blanched almond flour

¼ cup (34 grams) brown rice flour

⅓ cup coconut sugar

2 tablespoons ground flaxseed

2 teaspoons baking powder

1 teaspoon baking soda

1 teaspoon ground cinnamon

¼ teaspoon sea salt

3 medium very ripe bananas, mashed well (about 1 cup)

⅓ cup grapeseed oil

1 large egg plus 1 large egg white, lightly beaten

1 teaspoon apple cider vinegar

1 teaspoon vanilla extract

½ cup chopped walnuts (optional)

Preheat the oven to 350°F. Line a 9x5-inch loaf pan with parchment paper, leaving a 2-inch overhang on all sides.

In a medium bowl, whisk together the teff flour, arrowroot starch, almond flour, brown rice flour, coconut sugar, flaxseed, baking powder, baking soda, cinnamon, and salt.

In a medium bowl, whisk the mashed bananas with the grapeseed oil, egg and egg white, vinegar, and vanilla. Pour the wet ingredients into the dry and stir to combine. Fold in the walnuts, if using.

Pour the batter into the parchment-lined loaf pan. Bake for about 40 minutes or until a knife inserted into the center of the loaf comes out clean. Cool the bread completely in the pan before removing and slicing with a serrated knife. Store the bread tightly wrapped in an airtight container.

....

Technique Tip: In my many adventures (and disasters!) in gluten-free baking, I've found that allowing quick breads to cool *completely* before slicing them is imperative to preserving their structure. Although it may be tempting to sneak a slice of hot banana bread warm from the oven, do yourself a favor and exercise patience! You'll have beautiful slices with much less crumble if you cut cooled bread.

....

Cinnamon Currant Biscuits

Makes 8 biscuits

Serve these grain-free biscuits as part of a brunch menu with jam or the Fig Spread on page 104. If you don't have currants, swap in raisins, dried blueberries, or chopped pitted dates.

2 cups (192 grams) blanched almond flour

1 ½ teaspoons ground cinnamon

1 teaspoon baking soda

¼ teaspoon sea salt

1 large egg

3 tablespoons honey

1 teaspoon finely grated orange zest

⅓ cup dried currants

Preheat the oven to 350°F. Line a baking sheet with parchment paper.

In a medium bowl, whisk together the almond flour, cinnamon, baking soda, and sea salt. In a separate bowl, whisk together the egg, honey, and orange zest. Using a wooden spoon or rubber spatula, stir the wet ingredients into the flour mixture. Continue to stir until a thick dough forms. The dough will be sticky. Stir in the currants.

On a sheet of parchment paper, pat the dough into a 6-inch square about ½-inch thick. Cut the square into quarters. Cut each quarter in half to form 8 rectangular biscuits. Place the biscuits 2 inches apart on the baking sheet.

Bake for about 12 minutes or until biscuits spring back lightly when touched. Cool completely before serving. Store in an airtight container.

Quick Tip: Wet your hands slightly if the dough sticks to them as you pat it out. If the knife sticks to the dough as you cut out the biscuits, run it under cold water and then make your cuts. You can use this trick for the Lavender Almond Tea Biscuits on page 95 as well.

Going Grain-Free

Almond flour is a miracle ingredient for those following a grain-free diet, making it possible to enjoy healthy treats without the grains. When I stopped eating gluten, I initially cut out all grains (including brown rice, quinoa, millet, and gluten-free oats) from my diet because my body was incapable of digesting them. Over time as my digestive system healed, I was able to add gluten-free whole grains back into my diet with moderation. If you find that you feel better eating grain-free, these biscuits and the Grain-Free Granola Balls on page 68 are two of my favorite no-grain treats.

Maple Nut Granola Bars

*Makes 12 — **Vegan***

Delicious and subtly sweet, these granola bars rely on maple syrup, dried fruit, and just a hint of molasses for their sweetness. Perfectly chewy and slightly sticky, they make a satiating breakfast on the go, afternoon nibble, or road trip snack.

1 cup pitted prunes

⅓ cup dark maple syrup

1 tablespoon blackstrap molasses

1 teaspoon ground cinnamon

1 teaspoon vanilla extract

Pinch of sea salt

2 ½ cups gluten-free rolled oats, divided

½ cup dried apricots, finely chopped

⅔ cup raw walnuts, pecans, or almonds (or a combination), roughly chopped

⅓ cup raw sunflower seeds

Preheat the oven to 325°F. Line an 8x8-inch baking dish with parchment paper, leaving a 2-inch overhang on 2 sides. In a heat-safe bowl, cover the prunes with hot water. Soak for 10 minutes. Drain and place in the bowl of a food processor fitted with the steel blade.

Add the maple syrup, molasses, cinnamon, vanilla, and salt. Process to form a thick paste, about 20 seconds, stopping to scrape down the sides of the bowl once or twice with a rubber spatula. Add 2 cups of the oats and pulse 8-10 times until the oats are coarsely chopped. Transfer the mixture to a large mixing bowl. Stir in the remaining ½ cup oats, nuts, dried apricots, and sunflower seeds.

Using slightly wet hands, press the mixture firmly and evenly into the parchment-lined baking dish until tightly packed. Bake for 25 minutes.

Cool the dish for 15 minutes at room temperature, then transfer to the freezer and chill until completely cooled, about 30 minutes. Cut into 12 bars. Store in an airtight container at room temperature.

More Nutritious Snack Ideas

Aim to pair carbohydrates with either fat or protein (or both) when you construct a snack. It will stick with you longer and keep your blood sugar from spiking. Throw together these fast and satiating snacks in a flash:

✓ Apple or orange slices sprinkled with cinnamon and paired with a handful of raw almonds

✓ Brown rice cakes or crackers spread with nut butter or hummus

✓ Roasted chicken breast slices with salsa and a few whole grain, gluten-free crackers

✓ Carrots and celery dipped in hummus or bean dip

✓ Trail mix made with raw nuts, seeds, and dried fruit

✓ Boiled eggs mashed with avocado and spread onto brown rice cakes or crackers

✓ Smoothies made with fruit, almond or rice milk, and a scoop of gluten-free protein powder

✓ Small portions of leftovers from last night's dinner

Sweet Potato & Millet Cornbread

Makes one 9x13 inch pan

This cornbread comes together in a flash once you have the sweet potato puree made, making it a perfect accompaniment to a weeknight dinner. The sweet potato lends moisture and an extra layer of sweetness to the bread.

1 large sweet potato, peeled and cut into 1-inch chunks

1 ½ cups (210 grams) gluten-free medium-grind cornmeal

½ cup (65 grams) millet flour

½ cup (54 grams) arrowroot starch

2 teaspoons baking powder

1 teaspoon baking soda

1 teaspoon sea salt

Pinch of ground cinnamon

½ cup unsweetened almond or rice milk

⅓ cup virgin coconut oil, melted (plus more for greasing the pan)

Scant ⅓ cup honey

2 large eggs

Preheat the oven to 350°F. Lightly oil a 9x13-inch baking dish with coconut oil.

Bring 1 inch of water to boil in a medium pot fitted with a steamer basket. Add the sweet potato chunks. Cover and steam until tender when pierced with a fork, about 15 minutes. Transfer the chunks to a medium bowl and mash with a fork or potato masher until very smooth. (Alternatively, puree in a food processor fitted with the steel blade.) Measure out 1 cup of the puree and set aside.

In a large bowl, whisk together the cornmeal, millet flour, arrowroot starch, baking powder, baking soda, sea salt, and cinnamon. In a medium bowl, whisk together the remaining ingredients along with the reserved cup of sweet potato puree. Whisk the wet ingredients into the dry until thoroughly combined. Pour the batter into the oiled pan and spread it out with a rubber spatula.

Bake for about 20 minutes until golden brown and a toothpick inserted comes out clean. Cool for at least 30 minutes before cutting into squares and serving. This cornbread is best on the day it is made.

Lavender Almond Tea Biscuits

Makes 8 biscuits

If you've never eaten baked goods with lavender before, you are missing out. Floral, earthy, and reminiscent of rosemary, dried lavender flowers lend an incredibly delicate flavor to scones, muffins, quick breads, and even pancakes. Look for edible dried lavender at natural food stores or specialty gourmet shops.

2 cups (192 grams) blanched almond flour

1 ½ teaspoons dried lavender flowers, finely chopped

1 teaspoon baking soda

¼ teaspoon sea salt

1 large egg

3 tablespoons honey

1 teaspoon finely grated lemon zest

Preheat the oven to 350°F. Line a baking sheet with parchment paper.

In a medium bowl, whisk together the almond flour, lavender, baking soda, and sea salt. In a separate bowl, whisk together egg, honey, and lemon zest. Using a wooden spoon or rubber spatula, stir the wet ingredients into the flour mixture. Continue to stir until a thick dough forms. The dough will be somewhat sticky.

On a sheet of parchment paper, pat the dough into a 6-inch diameter disk about ½-inch thick. Cut into 8 wedges. Place the wedges 2 inches apart on the parchment-lined baking sheet.

Bake for about 12 minutes or until golden brown and biscuits spring back lightly when touched. Cool completely before serving. Store in an airtight container.

Variation: Can't find dried lavender flowers? Substitute 1 tablespoon of finely chopped fresh rosemary, increase the lemon zest to 2 teaspoons, and you'll have Lemon Rosemary Tea Biscuits.

Grain-Free Herbed "Pretzels"

Makes 8

These gluten-free, grain-free, dairy-free, yeast-free "pretzels" are a fun twist on traditional soft pretzels. The dough is very forgiving and can easily be pinched back into shape if it cracks or breaks in the shaping process. I love the pretzels plain, but you could also serve them with grainy mustard or tomato sauce for dipping.

2 cups (192 grams) blanched almond flour

1 ½ teaspoons Italian seasoning

1 teaspoon baking soda

½ teaspoon granulated garlic powder

¼ teaspoon sea salt

1 large egg

1 tablespoon agave nectar

Coarse salt, for sprinkling

Preheat the oven to 350°F. Line a baking sheet with parchment paper.

In a large mixing bowl, whisk together the almond flour, Italian seasoning, baking soda, granulated garlic, and sea salt. In a small bowl, separately whisk together the egg and agave nectar. Stir the egg mixture into the flour mixture until a thick dough forms.

Divide the dough into 8 equally sized portions. On a flat surface or sheet of parchment paper, roll each portion of dough into a 10-inch long rope. Fold the rope into a pretzel shape, pinching any cracks or breaks back together. Place the pretzels 2 inches apart on the parchment-lined baking sheet and sprinkle with coarse salt.

Bake for 8-10 minutes until lightly browned and just firm to the touch. Cool completely before serving.

....

Ingredient Tip: I ran out of Italian seasoning once while testing this recipe, so I swapped in poultry seasoning instead. The pretzels turned out equally delicious!

....

Buckwheat & Olive Oil Flatbread

Makes 15 flatbread squares

Perfect with a bowl of hot soup or spicy curry, this hearty yeasted flatbread bakes up beautifully. Try whisking finely chopped rosemary or oregano along with granulated garlic powder into the dry ingredients for an herbed variation.

1 tablespoon ground flaxseed

2 tablespoons boiling hot water

½ cup warm water (about 110°F)

2 tablespoons agave nectar or honey

2 (¼-ounce) packages active dry yeast

1 cup (120 grams) buckwheat flour

⅔ cup (70 grams) tapioca starch

½ cup (48 grams) blanched almond flour

½ teaspoon sea salt

2 large eggs

3 tablespoons extra-virgin olive oil, divided

In a small bowl, vigorously whisk together the flaxseed and boiling water to form a slurry. Set aside to thicken.

Place the warm water and agave nectar in a small bowl. Sprinkle the yeast over the water and stir gently to combine. Set aside for about 5 minutes until the mixture is foamy.

In a large mixing bowl, whisk together the buckwheat flour, tapioca flour, almond flour, and sea salt. In a separate bowl, whisk together the eggs and 2 tablespoons of the olive oil. Whisk the flaxseed slurry into the egg mixture. Add it to the flour mixture along with the yeasty water. Stir well with a rubber spatula.

Grease a 9x13-inch glass baking dish with the remaining tablespoon of olive oil. Transfer the batter to the dish and spread it out using the rubber spatula. Cover the dish loosely with a clean kitchen towel and set aside in a warm place to rise for about 40 minutes. Preheat the oven to 375°F.

Bake the flatbread, uncovered, for 12-15 minutes or until firm to the touch. Cool in the pan for at least 20 minutes before cutting into squares and serving.

Nourishing Nibbles

'm convinced that eating between meals is one of the easiest but least prac-
ticed methods of maintaining an optimal weight, balanced blood sugar,
and steady energy levels. In my experience working at a holistic healthcare
center, my jaw never failed to drop upon scanning the diet diaries of patients
who would literally go from nine o'clock in the morning until four o'clock in the
afternoon without one bite of food. By dinnertime, then starved for calories, their
stomachs would groan for anything and everything in sight, leading to poor
food choices all night long.

Snacks make my world go round. Munching on nuts in between meals or
grabbing a quick scoop of hummus with some vegetables provides my body
with a constant stream of fuel to function well throughout the day. I consider
snacks to be the backbone of "high performance eating," or eating to perform at
my very best level mentally, physically, and emotionally. Nibbling throughout the
day leads to better portion control at mealtimes, improved mood, and sustained
energy to power me through physical activity.

My love of snacks could quite easily have taken over this entire book, but I
limited myself to one section devoted to healthy nibbles. These recipes span a
variety of taste and texture profiles. If you find yourself in the mood for something
sweet and chewy, go with a granola bar or cluster of trail mix. For a veggie
fix, kale chips are a no-brainer. Pack a protein punch with a light but satisfying
salmon roll-up or a few Greek chicken meatballs. Whatever you choose, I'm
confident that the recipes in this section will extend you a warm welcome to the
wonderful world of snacking. 🖋

Fiesta Guacamole

Makes about 1 ½ cups — **Vegan, nut-free**

Guacamole is the quintessential party dip. And it just so happens to by my favorite. This variation glams up basic guac with tomatoes, corn, peppers, scallions, and cilantro. Serve it with a platter of fresh vegetables for dipping, or as a topping for the Black Bean & Quinoa Patties on page 190.

2 medium ripe avocados, halved and pitted

1 Roma tomato, seeded and chopped small

½ cup frozen corn, thawed

1 Serrano pepper, seeded and finely chopped (optional)

¼ cup finely chopped scallions (white and green parts)

¼ cup finely chopped cilantro

2 tablespoons fresh lime juice

½ teaspoon granulated garlic powder

Sea salt, to taste

Scoop the flesh of the avocados into a medium bowl. Mash with a fork until smooth. Stir in the tomato, corn, pepper (if using), scallions, cilantro, lime juice, and garlic powder. Season to taste with salt and serve right away.

Pumpkin Seed Pesto

Makes about ¾ cup of thick pesto — **Vegan, nut-free**

Tossed with brown rice noodles and sautéed kale, spread onto Buckwheat & Olive Oil Flatbread (page 97), or rolled up into an omelet with veggies, this pesto lends itself to a host of different uses. The secret lies in toasting the pumpkin seeds, which brings out their nutty quality and greatly enhances the flavor of the spread. See page 231 for a guide to toasting nuts and seeds.

1 cup (packed) flat-leaf parsley

½ cup (packed) fresh basil

½ cup pumpkin seeds, toasted

1 garlic clove

¼ cup water

3 tablespoons extra-virgin olive oil

2 tablespoons fresh lemon juice

Sea salt and black pepper, to taste

Combine all of the ingredients in a food processor fitted with the steel blade. Process until smooth, stopping once or twice to scrape down the sides of the bowl with a rubber spatula. Refrigerate in an airtight container until ready to use.

Variation: Swap in ½ cup toasted walnuts for the pumpkin seeds and ½ cup (packed) fresh cilantro for the basil. You'll have Cilantro Walnut Pesto, a tasty condiment for turkey burgers and grilled fish.

....

Flavor Heroes

Need a quick boost of fresh flavor or a fast but fab garnish?
Reach for herbs! I've come to call them "flavor heroes" because they
never fail to come to the rescue when I have a lackluster dish on my
hands. Add Mediterranean flair with basil, oregano, and rosemary.
Develop authentic Mexican flavor with cilantro and lime juice.
Or try using dill and chives for a little taste of France.

....

Pesto Hummus

Makes 1 ½ cups — **Vegan, nut-free**

One of my favorite afternoon snacks is a plate of carrot and cucumber slices with hummus and a few olives. This twist on traditional hummus is easy to whip up when you have Pumpkin Seed Pesto on hand, or feel free to use your favorite pesto in its place.

1 (15-ounce) can chickpeas, rinsed and drained

½ cup Pumpkin Seed Pesto (page 101)

1 tablespoon fresh lemon juice

1 teaspoon ground cumin

1 garlic clove

Sea salt, to taste

Combine all of the ingredients in a food processor fitted with the steel blade. Process until thick and smooth, stopping once or twice to scrape down the sides of the bowl with a rubber spatula.

Refrigerate in an airtight container until ready to use.

Stone Fruit Salsa

Makes about 2 heaping cups — **Vegan, nut-free**

Fruit salsas add punch and pizzazz to just about any summer meal. I like to serve this one over grilled fish or chicken, but it's equally delicious as a unique condiment to put out with corn tortilla chips. If peaches or apricots are unavailable, swap in fresh plums, nectarines, or pitted cherries.

¼ cup dried cherries, preferably fruit juice sweetened

2 medium firm but ripe peaches, pitted and chopped small

2 medium firm but ripe apricots, pitted and chopped small

1 small Serrano pepper, seeded and finely chopped

2 tablespoon fresh lime juice

1 tablespoon agave nectar

2 teaspoons extra-virgin olive oil

Pinch of sea salt

In a small bowl, cover the dried cherries with hot water and set aside to soak for about 5 minutes. Drain well and roughly chop.

Combine the cherries with the remaining ingredients in a medium bowl. Toss gently. Serve right away, or refrigerate in an airtight container for up to 4 hours before serving.

Fig Spread

Makes about 2 cups – **Egg-free, nut-free**

Earthy with a mellow sweetness, dried Black Mission figs are my weakness. Rarely can I stroll through the bulk bin section of my grocery store without picking up a bag. Here they're simmered with cinnamon and honey, then pureed into a spread that makes a sublime topping for quick breads and muffins. Try a dollop on roasted chicken breasts or turkey as well. My favorite way to enjoy it? Straight from the jar with a spoon.

10 ounces dried Black Mission figs, stemmed and chopped small (about 2 cups)

1 ½ cups water, plus ¼ cup more if needed

2 tablespoons honey

1 cinnamon stick

1 tablespoon fresh lemon juice

Bring the figs, 1 ½ cups water, honey, and cinnamon stick to a boil in a medium pot over high heat. Reduce the heat to low, cover, and simmer until most of the liquid has evaporated and the figs are tender, 18-20 minutes. Remove and discard the cinnamon stick.

Transfer the fig mixture to a food processor fitted with the steel blade. Add the lemon juice and process until smooth, adding up to ¼ cup more water if desired to thin out the spread. Store in the refrigerator in an airtight container for up to 1 week.

....

Cross Contamination in the Bulk Bins

Shopping from the bulk bins saves money and offers the opportunity to try new ingredients in small quantities. For those with severe gluten sensitivities, however, cross contamination is a valid issue to consider when buying bulk items. Because gluten-containing products (flour, pasta, granola, and the like) are often stocked directly next to gluten-free items such as brown rice or dried fruit, cross contamination can occur easily. Those with severe sensitivities or celiac disease are best off avoiding the bulk bins for this reason.

....

Crunchy Crackers

Yield will vary depending on the size you cut your crackers

I would venture to say that these crackers make an irresistible accompaniment to just about any meal. Savor them with your favorite soup, salad, dip, or salsa. Try adding dried herbs to the dry ingredients for even more savory flavor.

¾ cup (72 grams) blanched almond flour

½ cup (52 grams) sorghum flour, plus a tablespoon or so more if needed

¼ cup (27 grams) arrowroot starch

½ teaspoon baking soda

½ teaspoon granulated garlic powder

½ teaspoon sea salt

2 tablespoons extra-virgin olive oil

1 large egg white

1 tablespoon agave nectar or dark maple syrup

Freshly ground black pepper, to taste

Preheat the oven to 350°F. In a food processor fitted with the steel blade, pulse the almond flour, ½ cup sorghum flour, arrowroot starch, baking soda, granulated garlic, and salt until combined.

In a small bowl, whisk together the olive oil, egg white, and agave nectar. Pour this mixture into the food processor with the dry ingredients and process just until a soft and malleable (but not sticky) dough forms. If the dough feels sticky, pulse in more sorghum flour 1 tablespoon at a time to achieve the proper consistency. Transfer the dough to a sheet of parchment paper. Pat it out into a thick rectangular shape and top with another sheet of parchment paper. Roll out the dough between the parchment paper until very thin or as close to 1/16-inch as possible.

Cut the rolled out dough into cracker shapes of desired size using a sharp knife or pizza cutter. Transfer the dough, parchment paper and all, to a baking sheet. Sprinkle with black pepper to taste and gently press the pepper into the dough.

Bake for 15-20 minutes until golden brown and crisp. Cool completely on the baking sheet before separating the crackers and serving or storing. (They will continue to crisp up as they cool.) Store in an airtight container.

Sesame Sticks

*Makes about 22 sticks — ***Vegan***

These cracker-like sticks strike a perfect balance between crunchy texture and buttery mouth-feel. Their sesame flavor would mesh quite nicely with a hummus and vegetable platter.

1 ½ cups (144 grams) blanched almond flour

¼ cup plus 2 tablespoons sesame seeds, divided

¼ cup raw pecans

½ teaspoon sea salt

2 tablespoons water

1 tablespoon extra-virgin olive oil

Preheat the oven to 350°F. In a food processor fitted with the steel blade, pulse the almond flour, ¼ cup of the sesame seeds, pecans, and salt until the pecans and seeds are finely ground. Transfer to a large mixing bowl and stir in the remaining 2 tablespoons sesame seeds.

In a small bowl, whisk together the water and olive oil. Add to the dry ingredients and stir until a dough forms. On a sheet of parchment paper, pat the dough into a tightly packed 7x5-inch rectangle. Place another sheet of parchment paper on top of the dough and, using a rolling pin, roll the dough between the sheets of paper into a larger rectangle roughly 9x12 inches in size and 1/8-inch thick.

Trim the jagged edges of the dough with a pizza cutter to form a neater rectangle. Using the pizza cutter, cut the dough in half lengthwise. Cut crosswise to form 1-inch wide sticks. Transfer the cut dough, parchment paper and all, to a rimmed baking sheet.

Bake the sticks for 14-16 minutes until light golden brown and firm to the touch. Gently run the pizza cutter or a sharp knife along the previously cut lines while the sticks are still hot. Cool the sticks completely on the baking sheet before removing. Store in an airtight container.

Two Step Tortilla Chips

Makes 3 ½ - 4 cups — **Vegan, nut-free**

In two simple steps, you can make your very own tortilla chips—no deep frying required! When I'm craving a salty, crunchy snack, kale chips win me over every time. But when I want an accompaniment to salsa, guacamole, or bean dip, I whip up a batch of these. They're also a great topping for chili.

6 (6-inch) gluten-free corn tortillas, cut into wedges

1 tablespoon extra-virgin olive oil

1 teaspoon ground cumin

½ teaspoon granulated garlic

¼ teaspoon chili powder

¼ teaspoon sea salt, or more to taste

Preheat the oven to 400°F. In a medium bowl, toss the tortilla wedges with the remaining ingredients to evenly coat them with the oil and spices.

Arrange the wedges in an even layer on a rimmed baking sheet. Bake for 8-10 minutes until golden brown and crispy. Cool and serve.

....

Change It Up: Play with the spices to find your own favorite blend. For a sweet take on tortilla chips, toss them with cinnamon and a bit of coconut sugar instead of the spices. (They pair beautifully with the Stone Fruit Salsa on page 103.)

....

Sea Salt & Vinegar Kale Chips

*Makes about 3 cups — ***Vegan, nut-free***

Kale chips hit the fan long before I set out to write this book. For months, everywhere I looked—blogs, books, celebrity cooking shows—kale chips appeared to be taking over the world. Convinced that they were just a fad and couldn't possibly be as addicting as everyone claimed they were, I made a batch one night to see for myself. I had half the pan polished off in a matter of minutes! Salty with just a whiff of acid from the vinegar, I can assure you that a batch of these will vanish soon after you pull them out of the oven.

1 large bunch curly kale, stems removed, leaves torn into bite-sized pieces (5 – 6 cups)

1 ½ tablespoons extra-virgin olive oil

1 tablespoon apple cider vinegar

Generous ¼ teaspoon sea salt

Preheat the oven to 375°F. In a large bowl, toss all of the ingredients together. Arrange the kale pieces in even layers on 2 rimmed baking sheets.

Bake for 10-12 minutes until the chips are deeply browned around the edges. Cool completely before serving.

....

> **Heads Up:** Kale chips go from deeply brown to burnt in a flash. Watch them closely! Also, to ensure the crispiest chips possible, thoroughly dry your kale leaves of any liquid using paper towels or a salad spinner.

....

Trail Mix Clusters

Makes 16 clusters

Trail mix is the ultimate portable snack that's easy to tote along when traveling, hiking, or going on road trips. This recipe packs all the goodness of trail mix into individual, chewy clusters perfect for little hands.

1 large egg white

1 tablespoon honey

1 cup raw walnuts, coarsely chopped

½ cup raw pumpkin seeds

¼ cup raw sunflower seeds

¼ cup raisins or dried currants

1 teaspoon ground cinnamon

½ teaspoon ground ginger

Pinch of sea salt

Preheat the oven to 350°F. Line a baking sheet with parchment paper.

In the bottom of a medium bowl, whisk together the egg white and honey until frothy. Add the remaining ingredients and mix well to thoroughly coat everything with the egg white mixture.

Spoon tablespoons of the nut mixture onto the parchment-lined baking sheet. Bake until deeply golden brown and fragrant, 15-18 minutes. Cool completely before serving or storing. Store in an airtight container.

Simple Spice-Roasted Nuts

Makes 2 cups — **Vegan**

Place a bowl of these nuts on the table at your next gathering and watch them disappear. Savory and rich with just enough salt to taste indulgent, they're a hit with just about everyone I know. Wrap them up in a jar tied with some festive ribbon for a quick hostess gift.

1 cup raw almonds

½ cup raw cashews

½ cup raw pecans

1 tablespoon extra-virgin olive oil

½ teaspoon chili powder

¼ teaspoon ground cumin

¼ teaspoon granulated garlic powder

¼ teaspoon sea salt

Pinch of ground cinnamon

Preheat the oven to 325°F. Line a rimmed baking sheet with parchment paper.

In a medium bowl, toss all of the ingredients together until the nuts are evenly coated with the oil and spices. Spread in an even layer on the baking sheet. Roast for 18-20 minutes, tossing once halfway through, until the nuts are toasted and fragrant.

Cool completely. Store in an airtight container at room temperature.

Quick Tip: These nuts add a superb punch of flavor to salads. Just chop them up and throw them on your favorite vegetable medley.

Go Nuts for Nuts!

Nuts are one of my "desert island" foods. I don't think I could last more than a day or two without them. Packed with heart-healthy fats that help to lower LDL ("bad") cholesterol and promote weight loss, they are nature's ultimate convenience food. Almonds, pecans, walnuts, and cashews offer a double whammy of both protein and fiber, therefore helping to balance blood sugar and keep you satisfied.

Go-Green Mini Stuffed Potatoes

Makes 16 mini stuffed potatoes — **Vegan, nut-free**

Go green in a whole new way with this tasty take on stuffed potatoes. Bite-sized but packed with nutrients, these potatoes are a delicious and satisfying appetizer to serve at parties or potlucks.

8 medium red potatoes, washed and dried

3 tablespoons extra-virgin olive oil, divided

2 large lacinato kale leaves, stems removed, leaves finely chopped (about 1½ cups)

1 ½ cups bite-sized broccoli florets

¼ cup water

3 medium scallions, finely chopped (white and green parts)

1 teaspoon granulated garlic powder

Sea salt and black pepper, to taste

Preheat the oven to 400°F. Arrange the potatoes on a rimmed baking sheet and rub with 1 tablespoon of the olive oil. Bake the potatoes until tender when pierced with a knife, about 40 minutes. Set aside to cool.

While the potatoes bake, place the kale, broccoli, and water in a medium pot set over medium-high heat. Bring to a rapid simmer and then reduce the heat to low, cover, and cook until the vegetables are bright green and the water is almost entirely evaporated, about 5 minutes. Transfer the steamed vegetables to a large mixing bowl, leaving any excess water behind. Add the scallions and granulated garlic.

When the potatoes are cool enough to handle, cut them in half lengthwise. Using a small spoon or melon baller, scoop out the inside of each potato, leaving a ¼-inch-thick border around the edge. Add the scooped out potato flesh and remaining 2 tablespoons of olive oil to the bowl with the vegetables. Use a potato masher to work the mixture into a chunky mash. Season to taste with salt and pepper.

Divide the filling evenly among the hollowed out potato halves. Arrange in a baking dish and cover. Return to the oven for 10-15 minutes to heat through.

Make-ahead Tip: The stuffed potatoes can be refrigerated for up to 1 day or frozen for up to 1 month before baking. To reheat from the refrigerator: bring the dish to room temperature. Bake, covered, at 400°F for 20-25 minutes. To reheat from frozen: thaw 24 hours in the refrigerator. Bring the dish to room temperature and bake, covered, at 400°F for 30-35 minutes.

Salmon Salad Collard Roll-Ups

Makes 8 roll-ups — **Egg-free, nut-free**

Sturdy collard greens make excellent wraps for a variety of fillings. I often stuff the blanched greens with salads like this one, but they're also delicious filled with hummus and crunchy vegetables or beans and rice.

8 large collard leaves

2 ½ cups cooked, flaked wild Alaskan salmon

2 medium Roma tomatoes, seeded and chopped small

½ cup finely chopped red bell pepper

¼ cup finely chopped scallions (white and green parts)

¼ cup frozen peas, thawed

2 tablespoons fresh lemon juice

1 tablespoon extra-virgin olive oil

1 tablespoon Dijon mustard

Sea salt and black pepper, to taste

First, trim the collard greens: trim the stem of each collard leaf to be even with the bottom of the leaf. If the stems running through the leaf are particularly thick near the bottom, trim them as follows: lay the leaf "wrong side up" on a cutting board. Hold a sharp paring knife parallel to the cutting board and carefully shave off the thick portion of the stem, taking care not to puncture the leaf or cut the stem out entirely. Repeat with the remaining leaves.

Blanch the collard greens: bring 1 inch of water to boil in a large (10-12 inch) skillet or sauté pan. Using a pair of tongs, submerge each collard leaf in the water for about 1 minute. Remove to a paper towel-lined plate. Repeat with the remaining leaves.

Make the salmon salad: combine the salmon, tomatoes, bell pepper, scallions, peas, lemon juice, olive oil, and mustard in a large bowl. Mix just to combine, taking care not to break up the salmon too much. Season to taste with salt and pepper.

Assemble the collard rolls: place a blanched collard leaf "wrong side up" on a work surface. Scoop 1/8th of the salmon salad onto the bottom third of the leaf. Fold the sides of the leaf over the top of the filling and roll it away from you (as you would a burrito) to completely encase the filling. Repeat with the remaining leaves and salad. Serve.

....

Make-ahead Tip: Blanch the collard greens up to
2 days in advance. Store in an airtight container in the refrigerator
until ready to use.

....

Greek Chicken Meatballs
with Creamy Tahini Sauce

Makes 16 meatballs and about 1 cup sauce — **Egg-free**

Some people cringe at tahini's bold flavor. I happen to love it. This creamy, rich sauce pairs beautifully with the meatballs but would also be delicious as a salad dressing or passed with a platter of grilled summer vegetables. If you don't care for tahini, simply serve the meatballs with your favorite salsa or tomato sauce.

FOR THE MEATBALLS:

1 pound ground chicken

¼ cup finely chopped red onion

2 tablespoons finely chopped flat-leaf parsley

1 tablespoon finely chopped fresh oregano

2 garlic cloves, minced or finely grated

¼ teaspoon sea salt

FOR THE SAUCE:

½ cup tahini

¼ canned coconut milk (full fat)

3 tablespoons water

3 tablespoons fresh lemon juice

1 tablespoon agave nectar

1 garlic clove

Sea salt and black pepper, to taste

Preheat the oven to 400°F. Line a rimmed baking sheet with parchment paper.

In a large mixing bowl, combine all of the ingredients for the meatballs using your hands. Form the mixture into 16 meatballs about 1½-inches in diameter. Arrange the meatballs on the baking sheet. Bake for 18-20 minutes until cooked through.

While the meatballs bake, make the sauce: combine all of the ingredients for the sauce in a blender. Blend on high until smooth.

Serve the meatballs hot or warm with the sauce on the side for drizzling or dipping.

....

Quick Tip: To ensure all of your meatballs are evenly sized, divide the chicken mixture into 4 sections in the bottom of the mixing bowl. Divide each section in half. Form 2 meatballs out of each section.

....

Savory Soups & Stews

On a given weeknight in late autumn or winter, you'll most likely find me huddled near a simmering pot on the stove wrapped up in warm socks and a sweater. Growing up in the upper Midwest has led me to fall in love with one-pot meals. Long winters, snowy evenings, and late springs provide the perfect opportunity to chase away the wintry chill with a pot of steaming, rib-sticking comfort food.

Soups and stews act as a vessel for packing in megawatt nutrition. Loaded with lean protein from meat or legumes and simmered with mineral-rich vegetables, I find that some of my healthiest and most well-balanced meals reveal themselves in the form of stew. And when it comes to entertaining, especially to a group of hungry Midwesterners, you really can't get more simple or satisfying than serving up piping hot bowls of chili or chicken noodle.

You'll find that most of the recipes in this section follow the same pattern. I start out by browning the protein and vegetables in a bit of oil, then add in the spices and stir them for a minute or two to develop their flavors. Next into the pot goes the liquid so that the components of the soup can cook and soften. Often I'll stir in fresh herbs or citrus zest at the end of the cooking time to add a vibrant layer of fresh flavor. This basic pattern yields a savory and nutritious meal every time. Tinker with the proteins, vegetables, and spices and you'll soon be crafting brand new recipes of your own.

Cream of Broccoli Soup

*Serves 4 — **Nut-free***

While the flavor of most soups improves and deepens with time, make this humble soup just before serving as it is best eaten right away. The high vegetable-to-liquid ratio yields a thick, creamy soup that's not too brothy.

2 tablespoons extra-virgin olive oil

1 medium yellow onion, chopped

4 heaping cups broccoli florets

1 pound Yukon Gold potatoes, peeled and cut into ½-inch chunks

4 garlic cloves, finely chopped

5 cups low-sodium chicken broth

1 tablespoon fresh lemon juice

2 teaspoons honey

Freshly grated nutmeg, to taste

Sea salt and black pepper, to taste

Heat the olive oil in a large soup pot or Dutch oven over medium heat. Add the onion and broccoli. Cook, stirring occasionally, for about 5 minutes or until the onion is soft. Add the potatoes and garlic. Cook, stirring, for 1 minute. Add the broth and bring the soup to a boil. Reduce the heat to medium-low, cover, and cook at a vigorous simmer for about 15 minutes or until the potatoes are tender.

Puree the soup using a handheld immersion blender. (Alternatively, puree the soup in batches in a regular blender. Use caution when pureeing hot liquids. Return the pureed soup to the pot.) Stir in the lemon juice and honey. Season the soup to taste with nutmeg, salt, and pepper. Serve.

....

Jazz It Up: Garnish bowls of the soup with
chopped flat-leaf parsley and toasted pine nuts
or slivered almonds.

....

Cumin-Scented Potato Leek Soup

Serves 4 — **Vegan, nut-free**

When you're not in the mood for anything fancy but still want a warming meal, this soup is just the ticket. The sweet and silky sautéed leeks and the buttery Yukon Gold potatoes are a winning pair. I prefer to serve the soup "lazy man's style" and leave it chunky (no pureeing required), but if you'd like a smoother, more delicate texture, you can puree it in a blender or with a handheld immersion blender after the potatoes are tender.

2 tablespoons extra-virgin olive oil

4 medium leeks, white and light green parts only, chopped (3 ½ - 4 cups)

4 garlic cloves, finely chopped

1 ½ teaspoons ground cumin

1 ½ pounds Yukon Gold potatoes, scrubbed and cut into ½-inch chunks

2 ½ cups low-sodium vegetable broth

2 cups water

¼ cup finely chopped flat-leaf parsley

Sea salt and black pepper, to taste

Heat the olive oil in a large soup pot or Dutch oven over medium heat. Add the leeks and cook, stirring occasionally, for about 5 minutes or until tender. Add the garlic and cumin. Stir for 1 minute. Add the potatoes and stir for another minute. Add the broth and water. Bring the soup to a boil, then reduce the heat to medium-low and simmer, covered, for 18-20 minutes until the potatoes are tender.

Stir in the parsley and season to taste with salt and pepper before serving.

Chard, Chickpea, & Vegetable Soup

Serves 4 — **Vegan, nut-free**

This super simple vegetable soup has become a weeknight staple for me year round. Easy to make but rich with garden-fresh flavor, I even serve it to guests when I'm short on time. Serve it with the Sweet Potato & Millet Cornbread on page 94 or the Buckwheat & Olive Oil Flatbread on page 97.

1 tablespoon extra-virgin olive oil

1 medium yellow onion, chopped

2 medium carrots, peeled and chopped

2 medium celery stalks, peeled and chopped

1 small red bell pepper, seeded and chopped

3 garlic cloves, finely chopped

1 teaspoon ground cumin

1 teaspoon paprika

¼ teaspoon ground cinnamon

1 (14 ½-ounce) can diced tomatoes

4 cups low-sodium vegetable broth

1 (15-ounce) can chickpeas, rinsed and drained

1 pound (about 1 large bunch) Swiss chard, thick stems discarded, leaves chopped

Sea salt and black pepper, to taste

Heat the olive oil over medium heat in a large pot or Dutch oven. Add the onion, carrots, celery, and bell pepper. Cook, stirring occasionally, for 6-8 minutes until the vegetables begin to soften. Add the garlic, cumin, paprika, and cinnamon. Cook, stirring, for 1 minute. Add the tomatoes and broth. Bring the soup to a boil, then reduce the heat to low and simmer for about 10 minutes.

Stir in the chickpeas and chard. Cook for about 5 minutes to heat through and wilt the chard. Season to taste with salt and pepper before serving.

....

Three Cheers for Chickpeas!

Aside from being an excellent source of vegetarian protein, chickpeas (also known as garbanzo beans) pack a big fiber punch, therefore helping to flush toxins from the body and improve digestive health. Their firm texture holds up well in soups, curries, and stews, while also lending toothsome bulk to salads.

....

Black Bean &
Butternut Squash Chili

Serves 4 — **Vegan, nut-free**

Rehydrated ancho chilies give this version of the classic stew a unique flavor that's not quite smoky and not quite sweet. Black beans add protein and extra fiber while the squash lends sweetness and loads of vitamin A.

3 dried ancho chilies, stemmed and seeded

3 cups low-sodium vegetable broth

1 tablespoon extra-virgin olive oil

1 medium onion, chopped

2 large carrots, peeled and chopped

2 medium celery stalks, peeled and chopped

1 medium butternut squash, peeled, seeded, and cut into ½-1inch cubes (about 4 cups)

4 cloves garlic, finely chopped

1 tablespoon chili powder

1 teaspoon ground cumin

½ teaspoon ground coriander

1 cup water

1 (14 ½-ounce) can fire-roasted diced tomatoes

1 (15-ounce) can black beans, rinsed and drained

½ cup frozen corn (no need to thaw)

2 tablespoons fresh lime juice

Sea salt, to taste

FOR TOPPING:

Chopped cilantro

Diced avocado

In a medium pot, bring the anchos and broth to a boil over high heat. Reduce the heat to low and simmer for 10 minutes to rehydrate the chilies. Transfer to a blender and puree until smooth. (Use caution when pureeing hot liquids). Set aside.

Heat the olive oil over medium heat in a large soup pot or Dutch oven. Add the onion, carrots, and celery. Cook, stirring often, for about 5 minutes. Add the squash, garlic, chili powder, cumin, and coriander. Stir for 1 minute. Add the water, tomatoes, and reserved ancho puree. Bring to a boil, then reduce the heat to low and simmer, covered, until the squash is tender, 15-20 minutes.

Stir in the beans, corn, and lime juice. Cook for a few minutes to heat through. Season to taste with salt. Serve bowls of the chili topped with the cilantro and diced avocado.

Swap It: Instead of the butternut squash, try using 4 cups of peeled and cubed sweet potatoes.

Moroccan Sweet Potato & Lentil Stew

Serves 4 — **Vegan, nut-free**

I never tire of warming soups and stews in the winter months. Rich with the flavors of curry and cumin, this one tops my list of favorites. If you don't have time to cook the lentils, swap in a can of rinsed and drained chickpeas instead.

2 tablespoons extra-virgin olive oil

2 teaspoons brown mustard seeds

2 large (or 3 medium) sweet potatoes, peeled and cut into 1-inch chunks

½ medium yellow onion, chopped

2 medium carrots, peeled and chopped

4 garlic cloves, finely chopped

1 tablespoon tomato paste

2 teaspoons ground cumin

1 teaspoon curry powder

½ teaspoon ground coriander

3 cups low-sodium vegetable broth

4 cups chopped kale (stems removed and discarded)

1 ½ cups cooked green lentils

Sea salt and black pepper, to taste

FOR TOPPING:

Finely chopped flat-leaf parsley

Raisins or dried currants

Heat the olive oil in a large pot or Dutch oven over medium heat. Add the mustard seeds, sweet potatoes, onion, and carrots. Cook, stirring occasionally, until the onion is tender, about 5 minutes. Add the garlic, tomato paste, cumin, curry powder, and coriander. Stir until the spices are fragrant, about 1 minute. Add the broth, increase the heat to high, and bring to a boil. Reduce heat to low, cover, and simmer until the potatoes are tender, 12-15 minutes.

Stir in the kale and lentils. Cook for 3-5 minutes to heat through and wilt the kale. Season to taste with salt and pepper. Serve bowls of the stew sprinkled with parsley and a few raisins.

How to Cook Lentils: Bring 1 cup of green lentils (also called De Puy or French lentils) to boil with several cups of water in a medium pot. Reduce the heat to medium-low and simmer until the lentils are just tender to bite but not falling apart, 20-30 minutes. Drain well and refrigerate until ready to use. (You'll have more cooked lentils than you need for this recipe. Save the leftovers for another use.)

Cauliflower Parsnip Soup *with* Spring Pesto Drizzle

Serves 4 — **Vegan**

Serve this soup in the spring when there's still a bit of winter chill in the air but you want something light and easy for dinner.

1 tablespoon extra-virgin olive oil

1 medium yellow onion, chopped

1 medium head cauliflower, chopped into big florets (about 4 cups)

1 pound parsnips, peeled and cut into ½-inch chunks

1 large Yukon Gold potato, peeled and cut into ½-inch chunks

5 cups water

Sea salt and black pepper, to taste

Freshly grated nutmeg, to taste

Spring Pesto Drizzle, for serving (recipe follows)

Heat the olive oil in a large soup pot or Dutch oven over medium heat. Add the onion and cauliflower. Cook, stirring occasionally, for 6-8 minutes. Add the parsnips, potato, and water. Increase the heat to high and bring the soup to a boil. Reduce the heat to a simmer, cover, and cook until the vegetables are tender, about 20 minutes. Remove from heat.

Using a handheld immersion blender, puree the soup until smooth. (Alternatively, puree the soup in a regular blender in batches until smooth. Use caution when puree-ing hot liquids. Return the pureed soup to the pot.) Season to taste with salt, pepper, and nutmeg.

Serve the soup in bowls with a spoonful of the pesto drizzled over the top.

Spring Pesto Drizzle

1 cup (packed) baby spinach

½ cup (packed) fresh chives

½ cup (packed) flat-leaf parsley

¼ cup slivered almonds, toasted

¼ cup water

3 tablespoons extra-virgin olive oil

2 tablespoons fresh lemon juice

1 garlic clove

Sea salt and black pepper, to taste

Combine all of the ingredients in a food processor fitted with the steel blade. Process until smooth, stopping once or twice to scrape down the sides of the bowl with a rubber spatula. Refrigerate in an airtight container until ready to use.

Technique Tip: See page 231 for a guide to toasting nuts.

Summer Vegetable Soup
with Turkey Meatballs

*Serves 4 — **Nut-free***

This is the soup to make on early autumn days when the first nip of fall sends you to the closet to dig out your favorite sweater. What better way to savor the last of summer's bounty and usher in a new season?

FOR THE MEATBALLS:

1 pound ground turkey thigh

⅓ cup quinoa flakes

1 large egg white

1 teaspoon poultry seasoning

¼ teaspoon sea salt

FOR THE CHOWDER:

2 tablespoons extra-virgin olive oil

3 medium ears of corn, kernels cut off

2 medium celery stalks, peeled and chopped

1 medium yellow onion, chopped

1 medium red bell pepper, seeded and chopped

1 pound Yukon Gold potatoes, peeled and cut into ½-inch chunks

3 garlic cloves, finely chopped

1 teaspoon ground cumin

3 cups low-sodium chicken broth

½ cup fresh or frozen peas

Sea salt and black pepper, to taste

Chopped flat-leaf parsley, for garnish

Combine all of the ingredients for the meatballs in a large bowl. Shape the mixture into 12 evenly sized meatballs. Refrigerate and proceed with the recipe.

Heat the olive oil in a large soup pot or Dutch oven over medium-high heat. Add the corn kernels, celery, onion, and bell pepper. Cook, stirring occasionally, for 8-10 minutes. Stir in the potatoes, garlic, and cumin. Cook for 1 minute. Add the chicken broth and bring the soup to a boil. Gently place the meatballs into the bubbling broth, reduce the heat to medium-low, cover, and cook at a rapid simmer for about 15 minutes or until the meatballs are cooked through and the potatoes are tender. Stir in the peas and cook for about 2 minutes to heat through.

Season to taste with salt and pepper. Garnish with parsley and serve.

Curried Turkey Noodle Soup

Serves 4 to 6 — **Egg-free, nut-free**

Move over, Chicken Noodle! This flavorful twist on the classic bowl of comfort food we all grew to love as kids is a nutritional powerhouse. Chock-full of lean protein from the turkey, complex carbohydrates from the whole grain noodles, and cancer-kicking cabbage and curry power, a big bowl of this soup will fight off even the fiercest winter cold.

1 ½ cups brown rice noodles, such as elbows or penne

2 tablespoons extra-virgin olive oil

1 pound ground turkey breast

2 large carrots, peeled and chopped

2 medium celery stalks, peeled and chopped

½ medium yellow onion, chopped

2 cups thinly sliced green cabbage

2 garlic cloves, finely chopped

2 teaspoons curry powder

1 teaspoon poultry seasoning

4 cups low-sodium chicken broth

½ cup frozen peas, thawed

½ cup chopped cilantro

Sea salt and black pepper, to taste

Cook the brown rice noodles according to the package directions. Drain, rinse with cold water, and set aside.

Heat the olive oil in a large soup pot or Dutch oven over medium heat. Add the ground turkey and cook until it is no longer pink, about 8-10 minutes, breaking it up with a wooden utensil. Add the carrots, celery, onion, and cabbage. Cook, stirring occasionally, for about 5 minutes.

Add the garlic, curry powder, and poultry seasoning. Stir for 1 minute. Add the chicken broth and bring the soup to a boil. Reduce the heat to low and simmer for about 10 minutes until the carrots are tender.

Stir in the peas, reserved cooked noodles, and cilantro. If desired, thin the soup out with up to 1 cup of water. Season to taste with salt and pepper before serving.

Build a Meal in a Bowl

Soup offers the healthy home cook with the perfect opportunity to pack all of the components of a well-balanced meal into one pot. Incorporate lean protein such as chicken, turkey, beef, beans, or lentils and healthy fat like olive or coconut oil. Add in lots of vegetables (whatever is in season) along with broth or water and some spices. Kaboom! You're well on your way to a nourishing, couldn't-be-simpler meal.

Meaty Chicken & Mushroom Stew

Serves 4 — **Egg-free, nut-free**

Mushrooms lend a hearty, beefy quality to soups, stews, sauces, and casseroles. In this stew, that beefiness is doubled with the use of both dried porcini mushrooms and fresh portabellas. Despite being lean and nutritious, a bowl of this stew will stick with you.

1 ounce dried porcini mushrooms

2 tablespoons extra-virgin olive oil, divided

1 pound boneless, skinless chicken breasts, cut into ½-inch pieces

1 medium yellow onion, chopped

2 medium celery stalks, peeled and chopped

6 ounces portabella mushrooms, chopped (about 2 large caps)

4 garlic cloves, finely chopped

1 tablespoon tomato paste

1 teaspoon poultry seasoning

1 (15-ounce) can diced tomatoes

1 ½ cups water

2 cups chopped kale (stems removed and discarded)

½ cup frozen peas, thawed (optional)

¼ cup finely chopped flat-leaf parsley

Sea salt and black pepper, to taste

Place the dried porcinis in a small pot and cover with several cups of water. Bring to a boil over high heat, then reduce the heat to low and simmer for about 10 minutes to rehydrate the mushrooms. Drain, reserving 1 cup of the liquid, and chop the mushrooms. Set aside.

Heat 1 tablespoon of the olive oil in a large Dutch oven or pot over medium-high heat. Add the chicken and cook, stirring once or twice, until lightly browned and no longer pink, 4-5 minutes. Remove the chicken from the pot. (It will not be fully cooked at this point.)

Reduce the heat to medium and add the remaining tablespoon of olive oil to the pot along with the onion, celery, and portabella mushrooms. Cook, stirring occasionally, for 5-6 minutes. Add the garlic, tomato paste, and poultry seasoning. Stir for 1 minute. Add the tomatoes, water, kale, reserved mushroom liquid and porcini mushrooms, and reserved chicken. Bring to a boil, then reduce the heat to low, cover, and simmer until the chicken is fully cooked, 5-10 minutes.

Stir in the peas (if using) and parsley. Season the stew to taste with salt and pepper before serving.

....

Flavor Tip: When you add the liquids to the pot, use a wooden utensil to scrape up the browned bits of chicken and vegetables on the bottom. Tons of flavor lives down there, so you want to loosen it up and use it to enhance your stew.

....

Asian-Style Noodle Bowls
with Beef & Vegetables

Serves 4 to 6 — **Egg-free, nut-free**

This quick-cooking soup is proof that you can create your own delicious ethnic food at home, no specialty markets required.

6 ounces brown rice spaghetti

1 tablespoon extra-virgin olive oil

3 cups thinly sliced Napa cabbage

4 ounces cremini mushrooms, chopped or thinly sliced (about 1 ½ cups)

6 scallions, white and green parts thinly sliced on an angle (about 1 cup)

2 medium carrots, peeled and shredded

3 garlic cloves, finely chopped

1 tablespoon finely grated fresh ginger root

3 cups low-sodium chicken or vegetable broth

1 cup frozen peas (no need to thaw)

8 ounces deli sliced roast beef, preferably organic and grass-fed, chopped

Sea salt, to taste

TOPPINGS:

Cilantro or flat-leaf parsley, finely chopped

Mint leaves, finely chopped

Sprouts (broccoli, radish, alfalfa, or bean)

Lime wedges, for serving

Cook the spaghetti according to the package directions. Drain, rinse with cold water, and set aside.

Heat olive oil in a large pot or Dutch oven over medium heat. Add the cabbage, mushrooms, scallions, and carrots. Cook, stirring occasionally, for 6-8 minutes. Add the garlic and ginger. Stir for 1 minute. Add the broth and bring to a boil. Stir in the peas, roast beef, and reserved cooked spaghetti. Cook for 2-3 minutes to heat through. Season to taste with salt.

Serve bowls of the soup topped with the cilantro, mint, and sprouts. Pass lime wedges at the table for squeezing into the soup.

....

Time-Saving Tip: Cook the noodles, chop the cabbage, mushrooms, and scallions, and shred the carrots up to a day in advance. When you're ready to make the soup, it will come together in a flash.

....

Hearty Beef, Millet, & Vegetable Stew

Serves 4 — **Egg-free, nut-free**

Hearty and belly-filling, this stew gets an added boost of vegetarian protein and fiber from the millet. Easy to digest and rich in B vitamins as well as iron and magnesium, millet's versatility lends itself well to soups, stews, casseroles, pilafs, and porridges.

1 tablespoon extra-virgin olive oil

½ pound lean grass-fed ground beef

1 medium yellow onion, chopped

2 medium carrots, peeled and chopped

2 medium celery stalks, peeled and chopped

3 garlic cloves, finely chopped

2 teaspoons Italian seasoning

1 teaspoon paprika

½ cup millet, rinsed and drained

1 (8-ounce) can tomato sauce

4 cups water

3 cups chopped kale (stems removed and discarded)

½ cup frozen peas (no need to thaw)

½ cup finely chopped flat-leaf parsley

Sea salt and black pepper to taste

Heat the oil in a large soup pot or Dutch oven over medium heat. Add the beef and break it up into crumbles using a wooden utensil. Cooking, stirring and crumbling up often, until browned, 4-5 minutes. Add the onion, carrots, and celery. Cook, stirring occasionally, for about 5 minutes or until the vegetables are tender.

Add the garlic, Italian seasoning, paprika, and millet. Stir for 1 minute. Add the tomato sauce and water. Increase the heat to high and bring to a boil. Then reduce the heat to low, cover, and simmer for about 20 minutes until the millet is just tender. Stir in the kale, peas, and parsley. Cook for 3-5 minutes. Season to taste with salt and pepper before serving.

Pizzoccheri Stew

*Serves 4 — **Vegan, nut-free***

Never underestimate the soul-satisfying power of a humble bowl of cabbage soup. A play on pizzoccheri—a traditional European dish comprised of cabbage, potatoes, and buckwheat pasta—this simple soup satisfies in a big way. As the cabbage wilts into the olive oil and simmers in the nutmeg-scented broth, it morphs into a silky, buttery mass that's made even creamier with the addition of the Yukon Gold potatoes.

2 tablespoons extra-virgin olive oil

1 medium yellow onion, chopped

1 medium green cabbage (1–1 ½ pounds), quartered, cored, and thinly sliced

1 pound Yukon Gold potatoes, peeled and cut into ½-inch chunks

4 garlic cloves, finely chopped

¼ teaspoon freshly grated nutmeg

4 cups low-sodium vegetable broth

2 tablespoons finely chopped flat-leaf parsley

1 tablespoon finely chopped fresh sage

Sea salt and black pepper, to taste

Heat the olive oil over medium heat in a large pot or Dutch oven. Add the onion and cabbage. Cook, stirring occasionally, until the onion is soft and the cabbage is wilted, 6-8 minutes. Add the potatoes, garlic, and nutmeg. Cook, stirring often, for about 2 minutes. Add the broth and bring the soup to a boil. Reduce the heat to medium-low and simmer, covered, for about 15 minutes or until the potatoes are tender.

Stir in the parsley and sage. Season to taste with salt and pepper before serving.

··

Cabbage: The Cruciferous King

Cabbage is a member of the cruciferous vegetable family including cauliflower, Brussels sprouts, broccoli, and kale. Extremely high in anticancer phytochemicals, cabbage is also anti-inflammatory and anti-bacterial. It helps to detoxify the body of toxins and carcinogens (cancer-causing compounds) while also blocking the growth of tumor cells.

··

Vibrant Salads & Sides

While belly-filling soups, hearty stews, and comforting baked goods bring out my warm and loving side, vegetables—in all their fresh, colorful glory—evoke my passion. I will quickly admit that I'm an enthusiastic vegetable lover, squeezing them into meals in every way that I can. Why do I love them so? Two reasons. First, just look at them. Squint your eyes at the farmers' market and you'll see a blurry treasure chest of ruby red, emerald green, muted orange, and sunshine yellow. I love treating my plate like a canvas. Vegetables are the perfect tools with which to paint my dinner plate.

Second, it takes next to no effort to make them taste good. A flavorful dressing, a few crunchy nuts, and you're on your way to a knock-out dish. When it comes to veggies, I maintain the belief that most people who say they "don't like vegetables" simply haven't had the pleasure of eating them prepared properly. Canned beets, slimy green bean casseroles, marshmallow-speckled sweet potatoes—they taste nothing like the real foods themselves! Bursting with naturally occurring phytochemicals and nutrient-packed pigments, produce—when it's fresh and seasonal—needs very little to make it shine.

If you're a fence-sitter when it comes to veggies, I hope that as you make the recipes in this section, you'll come to see them in a new light and grow to love them as much as I do. Vegetables, the heartbeat of pure cooking and the densest source of nutrients available to us on this planet, deserve a prominent position in every pure eater's kitchen.

Arugula & Fennel Salad with Warm Orange-Balsamic Dressing

*Serves 4 — **Vegan***

My mom used to make a version of this dressing for her stand-by potluck salad with greens, walnuts, and goat cheese when I was growing up. It was always a smash hit. Her version had a fair bit of brown sugar in it, but I've found that by reducing the vinegar on the stove the sweetness becomes concentrated and you really don't need any sugar at all.

5 – 6 cups baby arugula

1 medium fennel bulb, quartered, cored, and thinly sliced

¼ cup balsamic vinegar

2 tablespoons extra-virgin olive oil

2 teaspoons Dijon mustard

2 teaspoons finely grated orange zest

Pinch of sea salt

1 orange, peeled and cut into segments

¼ cup pine nuts or slivered almonds, toasted

In a large bowl, toss together the arugula and fennel. In a small pot over medium-high heat, bring the balsamic vinegar to a boil. Cook until reduced and syrupy, about 3 minutes, swirling the pot occasionally to keep the vinegar from scorching. Remove from the heat and whisk in the olive oil, mustard, orange zest, and sea salt until emulsified.

Pour the warm dressing over the arugula mixture and toss to coat. Garnish with the orange segments and pine nuts. Serve immediately.

Technique Tip: See page 231 for a
guide to toasting nuts.

Fabulous Fennel

Fennel has long been attributed to stimulating the appetite,
aiding in digestion, and cleansing the palate. It's bright, licorice-like
flavor pairs beautifully with fresh fruit. When used raw in salads
and side dishes, it offers distinctive flavor and crunch that will
leave you wanting another bite.

Creamy Kale Salad

*Serves 4 — **Vegan***

Of all the salads in this book, there's a good chance that this one is my very favorite. Before going dairy-free, I used to make a creamy, slightly tangy coleslaw tossed with a mustardy sour cream dressing. This salad of crunchy kale dressed with a creamless but entirely luscious avocado dressing blows that old coleslaw out of the water. Serve it alongside grilled chicken breasts or the Vegan Sloppy Joe Bowls on page 192 for a delicious meal with megawatt nutrition.

6 cups thinly sliced lacinato kale (stems removed and discarded)

2 medium carrots, peeled and shredded (about 1 cup)

1 medium shallot, finely chopped

1 medium ripe avocado, halved and pitted

3 tablespoons water

3 tablespoons fresh lemon juice

2 tablespoons extra-virgin olive oil

1 tablespoon Dijon mustard

1 tablespoon dark maple syrup

Sea salt and black pepper, to taste

2 tablespoons sliced or slivered almonds, toasted

In a large mixing bowl, toss together the kale, carrots, and shallot.

Scoop the avocado flesh into a blender and add the water, lemon juice, olive oil, mustard, and maple syrup. Blend on high until smooth and creamy. The dressing will be thick with the consistency of mayonnaise.

Toss the dressing with the salad ingredients to coat evenly. Season to taste with salt and pepper. Let stand at room temperature for 15 minutes. Sprinkle the salad with the slivered almonds just before serving.

Shopping Tip: I like to buy more avocados than I need when I'm picking them up for recipes. This way, if I cut into one and it's an icky brown color, I have a back-up.

Technique Tip: See page 231 for a guide to toasting nuts.

The Awesome Avocado

Avocados, a rich source of monounsaturated fats that may help to lower LDL ("bad") cholesterol levels, also provide a good source of vitamin E and more potassium per gram than bananas. For those following a dairy-free diet, avocados mimic the creaminess of mayonnaise or yogurt in salad dressings, desserts, and smoothies.

Mixed Greens
with Pears & Grilled Onions

Serves 4 — **Egg-free, nut-free**

Sweet and soft, grilled onions are one of my favorite toppings for a simple mixed green salad. They dress it up, heightening it to a level worthy of entertaining, but certainly easy enough to plate up on a weeknight, too. The light and lemony dressing also pairs beautifully with steamed asparagus or baby carrots in the spring.

1 medium yellow onion, cut into ¼-inch thick rings

3 tablespoons extra-virgin olive oil, divided

Sea salt, to taste

6 cups mixed baby greens

1 medium ripe Bartlett pear, cored, quartered, and thinly sliced

2 tablespoons fresh lemon juice

1 tablespoon honey or dark maple syrup

1 tablespoon finely chopped flat-leaf parsley

Preheat a grill or grill pan over medium heat. Arrange the onion rings on a plate and brush both sides with 1 tablespoon of the olive oil. Sprinkle with salt to taste. Grill the onions until soft and lightly marked, 5-6 minutes per side.

While the onions cook, toss the greens and pear slices in a large salad bowl. In a small bowl, whisk together the remaining 2 tablespoons of olive oil, lemon juice, honey, parsley, and a pinch of salt. Top the greens with the grilled onions. Drizzle the dressing over the salad, toss to coat, and serve.

··

Mix It Up: Try apple slices or sliced Black Mission
figs instead of the pear.

··

Colorful Coleslaw

Serves 4 to 6 — **Vegan, nut-free**

This vibrant slaw makes a striking addition to a potluck or picnic spread. Serve it with burgers or other grilled fare for a classic summer meal.

4 cups thinly sliced green cabbage

2 cups thinly sliced red cabbage

2 medium carrots, peeled and shredded

½ cup thinly sliced scallions (white and green parts)

⅓ cup raisins or dried currants

¼ cup sunflower or pumpkin seeds, toasted

3 tablespoons extra-virgin olive oil

2 tablespoons apple cider vinegar

1 heaping tablespoon stone-ground mustard

1 heaping tablespoon agave nectar or dark maple syrup

2 tablespoons finely chopped flat-leaf parsley

½ teaspoon ground cumin

Sea salt and black pepper, to taste

In a large bowl, combine the green and red cabbage, carrots, scallions, raisins, and sunflower seeds. In a smaller bowl, whisk together the olive oil, vinegar, mustard, agave nectar, parsley, and cumin. Pour the dressing over the vegetable mixture and toss to combine. Season to taste with salt and pepper.

Cover and refrigerate for at least 1 hour before serving.

....

Technique Tip: See page 231 for a
guide to toasting seeds.

....

Shredded Balsamic Beet & Kale Salad

Serves 4 — **Vegan, nut-free**

Beets lend themselves well to a host of cooking methods. Roasted, pureed, steamed—you name it. But in my opinion, nothing is better than a simple salad of raw shredded beets and kale. The balsamic vinegar brings out their natural sweetness while keeping the beets raw preserves their vibrant color and nutrients.

4 medium red beets (about 1 pound), peeled and shredded

3 cups (packed) thinly sliced kale leaves (stems removed and discarded)

1 medium shallot, finely chopped

1 ½ tablespoons extra-virgin olive oil

1 ½ tablespoons balsamic vinegar

1 tablespoon Dijon mustard

½ teaspoon granulated garlic powder

Sea salt and black pepper, to taste

In a large mixing bowl, toss together beets, kale, and shallot. In a separate bowl, whisk together the olive oil, vinegar, mustard, and granulated garlic powder. Pour the dressing over the salad and toss to coat. Season to taste with salt and pepper.

Allow the salad to stand at room temperature for 15-20 minutes before serving.

Ingredient Tip: Try different types of kale in this recipe to find your favorite. I like lacinato kale the best for its flatter texture, but curly or red kale will also work.

Beautiful Beets

The jewels of the root vegetable treasure chest, beets are renowned for their earthy sweetness and jaw-dropping color. High in fiber, iron, and cancer-kicking antioxidants, beets offer an incredible line up of nutrients in a delicious package. Use fresh beets whenever you can as they are more nutritious, less sugary, and have less sodium than canned.

Herbed Whole Grain
& Asparagus Salad
with Lemon Vinaigrette

Serves 4 — **Vegan, nut-free**

Flavorful salads like this one are a great use-up for leftover cooked whole grains. I'll often cook up a big pot of quinoa or brown rice and use it throughout the week in salads, soups, stir-fries, or hot cereals. See page 229 for a guide to cooking whole grains.

1 bunch asparagus (about 1 pound), trimmed of woody stems

3 – 4 cups cooked and cooled quinoa, brown rice, or millet

½ cup frozen peas, thawed

¼ cup finely chopped flat-leaf parsley

2 tablespoons finely chopped fresh dill

2 tablespoons extra-virgin olive oil

2 tablespoons fresh lemon juice

2 teaspoons finely grated lemon zest

1 garlic clove, finely grated or minced

1 tablespoon dark maple syrup

Sea salt and black pepper, to taste

Cut the asparagus on an angle into 1-inch pieces. Place in a medium pot with about ½-inch of water and bring to a rapid simmer. Reduce the heat to low, cover, and cook for 4-6 minutes until the asparagus is just tender to bite. Drain and transfer to a large mixing bowl. Stir in your grain of choice, peas, parsley, and dill.

In a small bowl, whisk together the olive oil, lemon juice, lemon zest, garlic, and maple syrup. Pour the dressing over the salad and toss to coat. Season to taste with salt and pepper. Serve at room temperature or chilled.

Swap It: If asparagus is not in season,
try trimmed green beans instead.

Peach, Fennel, & Baby Green Salad
with Toasted Hazelnuts

Serves 4 — **Egg-free**

Sweet and crunchy, this dish captures the flavors of summer in a mouthwatering seasonal salad. If peaches are unavailable, swap in ripe nectarines, plums, or pitted cherries.

⅓ cup raw hazelnuts

5 – 6 cups mixed baby greens

1 medium fennel bulb, quartered, cored, and thinly sliced

1 medium shallot, thinly sliced

1 medium firm but ripe peach, pitted and thinly sliced

2 tablespoons extra-virgin olive oil

1 tablespoon apple cider vinegar

1 tablespoon honey

1 tablespoon finely chopped fresh thyme

Freshly grated nutmeg, to taste

Sea salt and black pepper, to taste

Preheat the oven to 350°F. Spread the hazelnuts on a rimmed baking sheet and bake for about 10 minutes until lightly toasted. When the nuts are cool enough to handle, use a paper towel to rub off the papery skins. Roughly chop the nuts and set aside.

In a large serving bowl, toss the greens, fennel, and shallot. Top with the peach slices and hazelnuts. In a small bowl, whisk together the remaining ingredients until emulsified. Pour the dressing over the salad and toss gently to coat. Serve immediately.

Quinoa, Black Bean, & Pineapple Salad

Serves 4 to 6 — **Vegan, nut-free**

Light and refreshing, this quinoa salad makes a tasty vegetarian offering for a summer potluck. For an equally delicious variation, swap in diced fresh mango for the pineapple.

1 cup quinoa, rinsed and drained

2 cups water

1 cup diced fresh pineapple

1 small red bell pepper, seeded and chopped small

1 (15-ounce) can black beans, rinsed and drained

¼ cup finely chopped flat-leaf parsley

2 tablespoons fresh lime juice

1 tablespoon extra-virgin olive oil

1 tablespoon agave nectar

1 garlic clove, finely grated or chopped

½ teaspoon ground cumin

Sea salt and black pepper, to taste

Bring the quinoa and water to a boil in a medium pot over high heat. Reduce the heat to low, cover, and simmer for about 15 minutes or until the water is absorbed and the quinoa is fluffy. Transfer the quinoa to a large mixing bowl, fluff it with a fork, and cool to room temperature.

Using the fork, stir the bell pepper, pineapple, black beans, and parsley into the quinoa. In a small bowl, whisk together the lime juice, olive oil, agave nectar, garlic, and cumin. Pour the dressing over the quinoa salad and toss gently to coat. Season to taste with salt and pepper.

Serve at room temperature or chilled.

Mediterranean Potato Salad

Serves 4 — **Vegan, nut-free**

I love a good potato salad, but have never been a fan of mayonnaise. This mayo-free version of the quintessential picnic side dish packs loads of flavor with a tangy Dijon vinaigrette and sweet red bell peppers.

2 pounds red potatoes, scrubbed and sliced into ¼-inch thick rounds

3 tablespoons extra-virgin olive oil

2 tablespoons red wine vinegar

2 tablespoons finely chopped flat-leaf parsley

1 medium shallot, finely chopped

2 teaspoons Dijon mustard

1 teaspoon granulated garlic powder

½ teaspoon dried oregano

½ cup jarred roasted red bell peppers, drained and thinly sliced

Sea salt and black pepper, to taste

Cover the potatoes with cold water in a large pot and bring to a boil over high heat. Reduce the heat to medium-low and cook until the potatoes are just tender when pierced with a knife, 8-10 minutes. Drain the potatoes well and transfer to a large mixing bowl.

In a medium bowl, whisk together the olive oil, vinegar, parsley, shallot, mustard, garlic powder, and oregano. Pour the dressing over the hot potatoes and toss gently to coat. Mix in the bell peppers and season to taste with salt and pepper.

Allow the salad to stand at room temperature until cool, about 20 minutes, before serving. The salad can be refrigerated for up to 1 day. Bring to room temperature before serving.

Lentil Salad
with Currants & Mint

Serves 4 — **Vegan, nut-free**

Behold the mighty lentil! Packed with protein, vitamins, and minerals, lentils are an inexpensive source of dense nutrition. Rich in fiber, they improve digestive health and may reduce the risk of colon cancer. My favorite way to enjoy them is in refreshing salads like this one. Fresh mint offers an unexpected and appetite-stimulating quality to the dish.

1 cup dry green lentils, rinsed and drained

1 cinnamon stick

2 medium celery stalks, peeled and finely chopped

2 medium Roma tomatoes, seeded and chopped

¼ cup finely chopped red onion

¼ cup finely chopped flat-leaf parsley

¼ cup dried currants

2 tablespoons finely chopped fresh mint

2 tablespoons extra-virgin olive oil

2 tablespoons red wine vinegar

½ teaspoon ground cumin

½ teaspoon granulated garlic powder

¼ teaspoon ground coriander

Sea salt and black pepper, to taste

In a medium pot, cover the lentils and cinnamon stick with water by 3 – 4 inches. Bring to a boil over high heat. Reduce the heat to medium-low, cover, and simmer until the lentils are just tender but not falling apart, about 20 minutes. Drain, rinse with cold water, and drain again. Remove the cinnamon stick and transfer the lentils to a large bowl.

Add the celery, tomatoes, onion, parsley, currants, and mint to the bowl with the lentils. In a small bowl, whisk together the olive oil, vinegar, cumin, garlic powder, and coriander. Pour the dressing over the salad and toss to coat. Season to taste with salt and pepper before serving.

Ingredient Tip: Green lentils are also called French or De Puy lentils.

Confetti Brown Rice Salad

Serves 4 — **Vegan, nut-free**

Take this vibrant, nutrient-dense salad to your next potluck or social gathering. Satisfying but light, it pairs well with just about any main dish. Feel free to vary the vegetables using what you have on hand.

2 ½ cups cooked brown rice

2 medium carrots, peeled and shredded

2 cups thinly sliced red cabbage

2 medium Roma tomatoes, seeded and chopped

4 medium Medjool dates, pitted and chopped small

¼ cup finely chopped red onion

¼ cup finely chopped flat-leaf parsley

2 tablespoons extra-virgin olive oil

1 ½ tablespoons red wine vinegar

1 tablespoon Dijon mustard

1 garlic clove, finely grated or minced

1 tablespoon agave nectar

Sea salt and black pepper, to taste

Combine the rice, carrots, cabbage, tomatoes, dates, onion, and parsley in a large mixing bowl. In a smaller bowl, whisk together the olive oil, vinegar, mustard, garlic, and agave nectar. Pour the dressing over the salad and toss to coat. Season to taste with salt and pepper. Serve the salad at room temperature.

....

Make It a Meal: Add cooked chickpeas or
cooked, chopped chicken breasts and serve the
salad over a bed of greens.

....

Sautéed Chard
with Dried Apricots

Serves 4 — **Vegan, nut-free**

I prefer sautéed chard over spinach, which tends to taste slimy if overcooked even just a little. Chard leaves, with their sturdier texture and thicker stems, retain a bit of crunch once cooked while still wilting easily.

2 bunches (about 2 pounds) Swiss chard, stems discarded, leaves chopped

1 tablespoon extra-virgin olive oil

1 medium shallot, finely chopped

⅓ cup dried apricots, chopped

1 tablespoon red wine vinegar

Freshly grated nutmeg, to taste

Sea salt and black pepper, to taste

Rinse the chard under cold water in a colander. Shake off excess water, but leave some still clinging to the leaves.

Heat the olive oil in a large skillet or sauté pan over medium-high heat. Add the shallot and cook, stirring often, for 2-3 minutes until soft. Add several big handfuls of the chard to the pan and stir to wilt it down. Continue adding more chard a few handfuls at a time until all of it fits into the pan. Cook the chard for 1-2 minutes until bright green and entirely wilted.

Remove the pan from the heat and stir in the apricots, vinegar, and freshly grated nutmeg to taste. Season with salt and pepper before serving.

Ingredient Tip: When you buy dried apricots, they should be brown, which indicates that they are unsulphured and natural. Bright orange apricots have been treated with sulphur dioxide to keep them lighter in color.

Go green, stay lean!

Loading your plate with dark leafy greens like chard, kale, and spinach is a surefire way to keep unwanted pounds at bay. Calorie for calorie, greens offer more nutritional density than any other food and are a low-carbohydrate side dish option. Pairing your greens with a little healthy fat (think olive oil or toasted nuts) helps your body absorb the vitamins and minerals more efficiently.

Maple-Glazed Root Vegetables

Serves 4 — **Vegan**

When I don't know what to make for a side dish to a winter meal, roasted root vegetables are my go-to choice. Here they are dressed up with a sweet maple glaze and some toasted almonds for buttery crunch.

1 ½ pounds rutabagas, peeled and cut into 1-inch chunks

1 ½ pounds turnips, peeled and cut into 1-inch chunks

6 medium carrots, peeled and cut into 1-inch chunks

1 tablespoon extra-virgin olive oil

Sea salt and black pepper, to taste

1 cup low-sodium vegetable broth

1 ½ tablespoons dark maple syrup

1 tablespoon balsamic vinegar

¼ cup sliced almonds, toasted

Preheat the oven to 400°F. Toss the rutabagas, turnips, carrots, and olive oil together with your hands on a rimmed baking sheet. Season with salt and pepper. Roast for 35-40 minutes until tender and brown in spots.

While the vegetables roast, make the glaze: bring the vegetable broth and maple syrup to a boil in a small pot over high heat. Reduce the heat to medium-low and cook at a rapid simmer until reduced to ¼ cup, about 20 minutes. Remove from the heat and stir in the vinegar.

Transfer the roasted vegetables to a serving dish. Drizzle with the glaze and toss to coat. Sprinkle with the almonds before serving.

....

Technique Tip: See page 231 for a
guide to toasting nuts.

....

....

Know Your Roots

Root vegetables are one of my many weaknesses at the
early autumn farmers' market. From deep ruby red beets to vibrant
carrots to knobby heirloom potatoes, root vegetables reel me in
with just one glance. Fall offers the perfect opportunity to try a
variety of roots as they flood into the market. Find your favorites and
stock up while you can. Root vegetables keep for months
when stored in a cool, dark room.

....

Skillet Green Beans
with Lemon & Tarragon

*Serves 4 —***Vegan**

The classic combination of green beans, lemon, and almonds is one of my favorite trios. If you blanch the green beans in advance, this dish comes together in less than ten minutes, making it the perfect last minute side dish to pair with just about any meal. Tarragon's bright licorice flavor does not set well with some people's palates, so feel free use less or omit it altogether if you prefer.

1 pound green beans, trimmed and thinly sliced crosswise into "O" shapes

1 tablespoon extra-virgin olive oil

½ medium yellow onion, finely chopped

3 garlic cloves, finely chopped

2 tablespoons finely chopped fresh tarragon

2 tablespoons finely chopped flat-leaf parsley

2 tablespoons fresh lemon juice

1 tablespoon finely grated lemon zest

¼ cup slivered almonds, toasted

Sea salt and black pepper, to taste

Bring a large pot of salted water to a boil. Add the green beans, bring the water back up to a boil, and cook for 2 minutes. Drain the beans in a colander, rinse with cold water, and drain again. Set aside. (At this point, the blanched green beans can be refrigerated in an airtight container for up to 2 days before proceeding with the recipe.)

In a medium skillet, heat the olive oil over medium heat. Add the onion and sauté until tender, about 5 minutes. Add the garlic and stir for 1 minute. Add the green beans, tarragon, and parsley. Cook to heat through, stirring often, for about 3 minutes.

Remove the pan from the heat and stir in the lemon juice, zest, and almonds. Season to taste with salt and pepper before serving.

....

Technique Tip: See page 231 for a
guide to toasting nuts.

....

Scallion Smashed Potatoes

Serves 4 — **Vegan, nut-free**

This couldn't-be-simpler side dish is perfect for a busy weeknight when you don't have time to make creamy but often laborious mashed potatoes. Because Yukon Golds are naturally buttery in flavor, they are the perfect choice for a quick smash like this one. The scallions add color and a garlicky note to the dish.

2 pounds Yukon Gold potatoes, peeled and cut into ½-inch chunks

½ cup finely chopped scallions (white and green parts)

3 tablespoons extra-virgin olive oil

Sea salt and black pepper, to taste

Place the potatoes in a medium pot and cover with cold water by several inches. Bring to a boil over high heat. Reduce the heat to medium and boil the potatoes until fork tender, about 20 minutes. Drain the potatoes in a colander and return them to the hot pot.

Add the scallions, olive oil, and salt and pepper to taste. Roughly smash the potatoes with a potato masher to yield a chunky texture. Serve.

....

Ingredient Tip: Scallions are also called
green onions or spring onions.

....

Moroccan Millet & Butternut Squash Pilaf

Serves 4 — **Vegan, nut-free**

This hearty whole grain pilaf makes a flavorful side dish to a festive autumn or winter meal. If butternut squash is unavailable, try using another sweet winter squash or sweet potatoes instead.

1 medium butternut squash, peeled, seeded, and cut into 1-inch cubes

2 tablespoons extra-virgin olive oil, divided

¼ teaspoon sea salt (plus more to taste)

½ medium yellow onion, finely chopped

2 garlic cloves, finely chopped

1 teaspoon brown mustard seeds

1 teaspoon ground cumin

1 teaspoon curry powder

1 cup millet, rinsed and drained

2 ¼ cups water

¼ cup dried currants

¼ cup pitted green olives, chopped

¼ cup finely chopped flat-leaf parsley

Preheat the oven to 400°F. On a rimmed baking sheet, toss the squash cubes with 1 tablespoon of the olive oil and ¼ teaspoon salt. Roast for 25-30 minutes until tender and brown in spots.

Meanwhile, heat the remaining tablespoon of olive oil in a medium pot over medium-low heat. Add the onion, garlic, and mustard seeds. Cook, stirring often, until the onion is soft and translucent, 3-5 minutes. Add the cumin, curry powder, and millet. Stir for 1 minute. Add the water. Increase the heat to high and bring to a boil. Cover, reduce the heat to low, and simmer until the water is absorbed and millet is fluffy, 25-30 minutes.

Using a fork, fluff up the millet and mix in the currants, olives, and parsley. Gently stir in the squash and season the pilaf to taste with salt before serving.

Pure Proteins

When it comes to main meals, I try to vary my protein sources as much as possible. Incorporating both plant-based, vegetarian dinners as well as those that are meat-centric strikes the perfect balance for me personally. I feel the best eating a "flexitarian diet" that incorporates both dense sources of animal protein in small amounts and plenty of nutrient-rich vegetables. Remember that when choosing animal foods, it's paramount to choose high-quality and organic options whenever possible.

In this section, you'll find a broad spectrum of protein dishes ranging in scope from easy roasted chicken strips to beef taco bowls to vegan Sloppy Joe's. While some of the recipes require more advance planning and prep time, others can be whipped up in a snap. On busy weeknights, I typically make something simple and stream-lined, or may even rely on my slow cooker for a hot meal with next to no prep work. If I have more time, I'll turn on some music, grab my trusty chef's knife, and go to town on a more elaborate but still nutritious meal.

Whatever your cooking style or time constraints, I hope the meals in this section inspire you take a few moments to slow down and enjoy the process of cooking and savoring a wholesome dinner. Gathering around the table at the end of a long day in the company of friends or family is the perfect way to refuel, refocus, and reenergize.

Honey Mustard Salmon
with Lemony Herbed Quinoa

Serves 4 — **Egg-free, nut-free**

Add a simple salad to this salmon supper for a well-balanced, light, and flavorful meal.

1 cup quinoa, rinsed and drained

2 cups water

3 tablespoons snipped or finely chopped chives

2 tablespoons finely chopped flat-leaf parsley

1 tablespoon fresh lemon juice

1 tablespoon finely grated lemon zest

Sea salt, to taste

3 tablespoons stone ground mustard

2 tablespoons honey

½ teaspoon caraway seeds

1 tablespoon extra-virgin olive oil

1 ½ pounds wild Alaskan salmon, cut into 4 pieces of equal size

Preheat the oven to 400°F. Bring the quinoa and water to a boil in a medium pot over high heat. Reduce the heat to low, cover, and simmer until the water is absorbed and the quinoa is fluffy, about 15 minutes. Remove from heat. Using a fork, gently mix in the chives, parsley, lemon juice and zest, and salt to taste. Cover to keep warm.

In a small bowl, combine the mustard, honey, caraway seeds, and a pinch of salt. Rub the salmon filets with the olive oil and place skin side down in a 9x13-inch glass baking dish. Spread the honey-mustard mixture over the salmon.

Bake for 12-15 minutes until the fish flakes easily when pricked with a fork, or to desired degree of doneness. Serve the salmon on a bed of the herbed quinoa.

....

Technique Tip: Always zest your
citrus before juicing it.

....

Italian Baked Cod
with Fennel, Tomatoes, & White Beans

Serves 4 — **Egg-free, nut-free**

Easy to make but super healthy, I like to serve this dish with brown rice and steamed broccoli for a beautiful balanced meal.

1 ½ tablespoons extra-virgin olive oil, divided

1 medium fennel bulb, quartered, cored, and thinly sliced

½ medium yellow onion, finely chopped

2 garlic cloves, finely chopped

1 teaspoon Italian seasoning

1 (14 ½-ounce) can diced tomatoes

1 (15-ounce) can cannellini or navy beans, rinsed and drained

Sea salt and black pepper, to taste

1 pound Pacific cod, cut into 4 pieces

Chopped fresh basil, for garnish

Preheat the oven to 400°F. Oil the bottom of a 9x12-inch baking dish with ½ tablespoon of the olive oil. Set aside.

Heat the remaining 1 tablespoon of olive oil in a medium pot over medium-high heat. Add the fennel and onion and cook, stirring occasionally, for 6-8 minutes. Add the garlic and Italian seasoning and stir for 1 minute. Add the tomatoes and beans. Cook for about 5 minutes to blend the flavors. Season to taste with salt and pepper.

Arrange the cod filets in the baking dish. Spoon the tomato-bean mixture over the filets. Cover the dish with a sheet of parchment paper and bake for about 15 minutes or until the fish is just cooked through. Garnish with the basil and serve.

....

Ingredient Tip: Be sure to purchase cod labeled "Pacific" or "Alaskan." Because Atlantic cod is often farmed and overfished, it is not a sustainable choice.

....

Coconut Fish & Cauliflower Curry

Serves 4 — **Egg-free**

I was never a fan of curry until I started making it at home. Often I find that people—especially kids—will happily gobble up ethnic food when it's tailored to their tastes. Cooking at home presents you with the perfect opportunity to control the heat and salt levels of a dish. Enjoy this mild curry spooned over cooked brown rice or quinoa for a hearty meal.

2 tablespoons virgin coconut oil

3 cups bite-sized cauliflower florets

1 medium yellow onion, chopped

2 medium carrots, peeled, halved lengthwise, and sliced thinly into half-moons

2 medium celery stalks, peeled and chopped

3 garlic cloves, finely chopped

2 teaspoons curry powder

1 teaspoon ground cumin

½ teaspoon ground coriander

1 (14 ½-ounce) can diced tomatoes

¾ cup water or low-sodium vegetable broth

¾-1 pound white fish such as halibut or mahi mahi, cut into 1-inch chunks

½ cup canned coconut milk (full fat)

2 tablespoons arrowroot starch

½ cup frozen peas, thawed

2 tablespoons fresh lime juice

Sea salt and black pepper, to taste

Chopped flat-leaf parsley or cilantro, for garnish

Heat the coconut oil over medium-high heat in a large sauté pan. Add the cauliflower, onion, carrots, and celery. Cook, stirring often, until the onion is soft and translucent, about 6 minutes. Add the garlic, curry powder, cumin, and coriander and stir for 1 minute. Add the tomatoes, water, and fish. Bring to a rapid simmer, then reduce the heat to low, cover, and simmer until the cauliflower is tender and fish is cooked through, about 10 minutes.

Whisk the coconut milk with the arrowroot starch in a small bowl to dissolve. Gently stir this mixture along with the peas and lime juice into the curry. Season to taste with salt and pepper. Do not stir it too much or the fish will break apart. Cook for 2-3 minutes to thicken the sauce. Garnish the curry with the parsley and serve.

....

Spice It Up! If you live for heat, use a hot curry powder such as Madras or sauté a chopped jalapeno pepper along with the other vegetables.

....

....

The Spice of Life

Curry powder derives its deep orange hue from turmeric, a ground root chock-full of a pigment called curcumin. Curcumin is known to be a potent anti-inflammatory and has also been shown to alleviate symptoms of irritable bowel syndrome (IBS) and rheumatoid arthritis. As if that weren't enough, curcumin delivers a mega dose of antioxidants that help to shrink tumors and prevent the formation of various cancers. For these reasons and because of its rich, spicy flavor, I'm a curry-lover through and through!

....

Lemon Herb-Baked Sole

Serves 4 — **Egg-free, nut-free**

Sometimes the simplest dishes are the most memorable and flavorful. When you have a good, fresh piece of fish, I maintain the belief that all you need to enhance it is a few herbs, a bit of citrus action, and some salt. Serve this sole with your favorite side dishes (almost anything goes here) and call it a day.

¼ cup finely chopped flat-leaf parsley

2 tablespoons extra-virgin olive oil

1 tablespoon finely chopped fresh oregano

2 garlic cloves, minced or finely grated

2 teaspoons finely grated lemon zest

½ teaspoon sea salt

8 (3 – 4 ounce) Pacific sole filets, patted dry

1 lemon, very thinly sliced

Preheat the oven to 375°F. In a small bowl, combine the parsley, olive oil, oregano, garlic, lemon zest, and salt. Arrange the sole filets in 1 large or 2 medium baking dishes. Rub the fish with the herb paste. Scatter the lemon slices over the fish.

Bake for 15-20 minutes or until the fish flakes easily when pricked with a fork. Serve immediately.

Seafood Savvy: Remember to choose wisely and go for quality when you select seafood. Look for Pacific, wild-caught sole or flounder filets.

Chicken Strips
with Maple-Mustard Dipper

Serves 4 — **Egg-free, nut-free**

This recipe received rave reviews from all of the moms in my recipe testing group. On busy weeknights, the chicken and sauce come together in no time. Kids love the sweetness of the maple syrup in the sauce, while dipping the chicken strips makes the meal interactive and fun. Serve it with the Scallion Smashed Potatoes on page 161 and a tossed salad for a wholesome meal everyone will love.

1 ½ pounds boneless, skinless chicken breasts, cut into 1-inch wide strips

¼ cup plus 1 tablespoon extra-virgin olive oil, divided

1 teaspoon poultry seasoning

½ teaspoon sea salt

½ cup Dijon mustard

¼ cup dark maple syrup

Black pepper, to taste

Preheat the oven to 400°F. On a rimmed baking sheet, toss together the chicken strips with 1 tablespoon of the olive oil, the poultry seasoning, and the salt. Arrange the strips in an even layer on the sheet and bake for 25-30 minutes until golden brown and cooked through.

Meanwhile, whisk together the remaining ¼ cup olive oil, mustard, maple syrup, and pepper to taste. Serve the chicken strips with the dipping sauce.

....

"Dipper Dinners"

Most kids will eat just about anything if they can dip it. "Dipper dinners" may include vegetables with hummus or nut butter, chicken strips with mustard, meatballs with salsa, or baked corn chips with bean spread. Dipping is an interactive way for little ones to engage with their food. And hey—who doesn't love eating with their fingers?

....

Slow-Cooker Indian Chicken with Quinoa

Serves 4 — **Egg-free**

Don't you love it when you just throw together a few hodge-podge ingredients and end up with a winning dinner? That's how this recipe came about. On the morning of a busy day, I threw some veggies, chicken, and spices in my slow-cooker, set it on low, and forgot about it. When I came home that night, I threw in some raisins for sweetness and coconut milk for creaminess. The result? Incredible Indian-style chicken and vegetables delicious served over a bowl of quinoa.

1 medium red bell pepper, seeded and chopped

3 medium carrots, peeled and cut into ¼-inch thick slices

1 medium yellow onion, chopped

1 ½ cups cremini mushrooms, quartered

6 boneless, skinless chicken thighs (about 1 ¼ pounds)

2 teaspoons curry powder

1 teaspoon granulated garlic powder

½ teaspoon sea salt

1 cup low-sodium chicken broth

⅓ cup canned coconut milk (full fat)

2 teaspoons arrowroot starch

⅓ cup raisins or dried currants

1 ¼ cups quinoa

2 ½ cups water

Chopped cilantro, for garnish

Place the bell pepper, carrots, onion, and mushrooms in the bottom of a large (4- to 6-quart) slow cooker. Rub the chicken thighs with the curry powder, garlic powder, and salt. Arrange on top of the vegetables. Pour the broth over the chicken. Cover and cook on low for 7-8 hours or on high for 4 hours.

In a small bowl, whisk together the coconut milk and arrowroot starch to combine. Stir the mixture into the chicken and vegetables along with the currants. Use 2 forks to shred up the chicken thighs in the bottom of the slow cooker. Cover and continue to cook on low for 30 minutes or on high for 15 minutes.

While the chicken finishes cooking, make the quinoa: bring the quinoa and water to boil in a medium pot over high heat. Reduce the heat to low, cover, and cook until the water is absorbed and the quinoa is fluffy, about 15 minutes.

Serve the chicken and vegetables over the quinoa. Garnish with the cilantro.

....

Chicken: Dark vs. White Meat

Using chicken thighs instead of breasts in slow cooker recipes ensures that they don't dry out during the long cooking process. Organic chicken thighs from pasture-raised birds are leaner than conventional and higher in nutrients.

....

Baked Chicken Thighs
with Balsamic Cherry Pan Sauce

Serves 4 — **Egg-free, nut-free**

This elegant but incredibly easy-to-make chicken dish is pretty much foolproof, but you'd never know it from the rich flavors. We all need impressive but effortless recipes like this one in our repertoire for entertaining and special occasions. For a complete meal, serve the chicken and sauce atop a bed of warm wild and brown rice. Serve it with a simple green salad and you've got yourself a meal guaranteed to reel in the praises!

1 ½ pounds boneless, skinless chicken thighs

2 tablespoons extra-virgin olive oil, divided

3 tablespoons balsamic vinegar, divided

½ teaspoon sea salt (plus more to taste)

½ teaspoon poultry seasoning

2 medium shallots, finely chopped

½ cup dried cherries, preferably fruit juice sweetened

¾ cup low-sodium chicken broth

2 tablespoons finely chopped fresh parsley

1 tablespoon finely chopped fresh thyme

Preheat the oven to 400°F. Toss the chicken thighs with 1 tablespoon of the olive oil, 1 tablespoon of the vinegar, ½ teaspoon sea salt, and poultry seasoning in a 9x13-inch glass baking dish. Arrange the thighs in an even layer in the dish. Cover loosely with a sheet of parchment paper and bake for 15 minutes. Remove parchment and continue baking for another 20 minutes or until the thighs are cooked through and golden brown.

Meanwhile, make the sauce: heat the remaining tablespoon of oil in a small pot over medium heat. Add the shallots and sauté for 3-5 minutes until tender. Add the dried cherries, chicken broth, and remaining 2 tablespoons vinegar. Simmer over medium-high heat for 4-5 minutes until the sauce has reduced and thickened. Stir in the parsley and thyme. Season to taste with salt.

Serve the sauce spooned over the baked chicken thighs.

Nutty Almond Chicken & Rice

Serves 4 — **Egg-free**

I originally developed this recipe for a cooking class I taught called "Gluten-Free Dinners in 5 Ingredients or Less." All of the students begged me to put this recipe in my cookbook, and for good reason! With just five ingredients (not including salt, olive oil, and water), the dish is wonderfully creamy, satisfying, and comes together in minutes.

⅓ cup creamy roasted almond butter

1 cup water

1 tablespoons extra-virgin olive oil

1 ¼ pound boneless, skinless chicken thighs, cut into 1-inch pieces

1 cup shredded carrots

1 cup thinly sliced scallions (white and green parts)

Sea salt, to taste

Cooked brown rice, for serving

In a small bowl, whisk together the almond butter and water. Set aside.

Heat the olive oil in a large sauté pan or Dutch oven over medium-high heat. Add the chicken and cook, stirring occasionally, for 8-10 minutes until browned and cooked through. Add the carrots and scallions. Cook, stirring often, for 2 minutes. Add the almond butter mixture. Cook for 2-3 minutes until the sauce has thickened and bubbles rapidly.

Season to taste with salt. Serve over brown rice.

....

Jazz It Up: Garnish the dish with toasted sliced almonds and chopped parsley.

....

....

Swap It: If you prefer the flavor of chicken breast meat over thigh meat, use an equal amount of boneless, skinless chicken breasts instead.

....

Middle Eastern Marinated Chicken with Warm Tomato Chutney

Serves 4 — **Egg-free**

Marinating the chicken in a blend of coconut milk, lemon juice and zest, and Middle Eastern spices ensures that it stays moist and tender in the oven. The sweet tomato chutney, a classic Mediterranean condiment, is also delicious spooned over steak or burgers.

FOR THE CHICKEN:

1 ½ pounds boneless, skinless chicken breasts

¾ cup canned coconut milk (full fat)

2 tablespoons fresh lemon juice

1 teaspoon finely grated lemon zest

4 garlic cloves, finely chopped or grated

1 ½ teaspoons ground cumin

¾ teaspoon ground coriander

½ teaspoon sea salt

FOR THE CHUTNEY:

1 tablespoon extra-virgin olive oil

1 teaspoon brown mustard seeds

1 medium shallot, finely chopped

1 cinnamon stick

4 cups chopped tomatoes

2 tablespoons honey

2 teaspoons finely grated fresh ginger root

Pinch of sea salt

2 tablespoons finely chopped flat-leaf parsley

Cut the chicken breasts in half crosswise to form palm-sized pieces. Whisk the coconut milk, lemon juice and zest, garlic, cumin, coriander, and salt in the bottom of a large mixing bowl. Add the chicken pieces and toss to coat. Cover and refrigerate for 4-8 hours.

Preheat the oven to 400°F. Remove the chicken pieces from the marinade. (Discard remaining marinade.) Arrange in an even layer in a 9x13-inch glass baking dish. Bake for 25-30 minutes until the chicken is cooked through and lightly browned.

While the chicken cooks, make the chutney: heat the olive oil in a medium pot over medium heat. Add the mustard seeds, shallot, and cinnamon stick. Cook, stirring occasionally, until the shallot is tender and translucent, about 3 minutes. Stir in the tomatoes, honey, ginger, and salt. Cook, stirring occasionally, until the tomatoes have broken down into a chunky sauce and the juices have reduced, 15-20 minutes. Remove from heat and stir in the parsley. (Chutney will keep in the refrigerator for up to 2 days. Reheat before serving.)

Serve the baked chicken with the chutney.

Asian-Style Turkey Burgers *with* Cucumber Sesame Salad

Serves 4 — **Egg-free, nut-free**

With their parsley, scallions, garlic, and ginger, these burgers not only burst with refreshing flavor, but the herbs and scallions also help to keep the lean turkey breast moist. The snappy cucumber salad adds another layer of texture and tang. Serve with the Colorful Coleslaw on page 147 and some roasted sweet potatoes.

FOR THE SALAD:

1 medium English cucumber, peeled (optional) and thinly sliced

2 tablespoons gluten-free brown rice vinegar

1 tablespoon sesame seeds

Pinch of sea salt

FOR THE BURGERS:

1 pound ground turkey breast

¼ cup finely chopped flat-leaf parsley

2 scallions, finely chopped (white and green parts)

2 garlic cloves, finely grated or minced

1 tablespoon finely grated fresh ginger root

½ teaspoon sea salt

1 tablespoon extra-virgin olive oil

Thinly sliced romaine lettuce, for serving

Combine all of the ingredients for the cucumber salad in a medium mixing bowl. Refrigerate and proceed with the recipe.

In a large mixing bowl, combine the turkey, parsley, scallions, garlic, ginger, and salt. Mix well with your hands and shape into four ½-inch thick patties. Brush a grill, grill pan, or large skillet with the olive oil and set it over medium-high heat. Heat up the pan for a minute or two, then add the burgers. Cook for 4-5 minutes per side until browned and cooked through.

To serve, arrange the lettuce on a large serving platter or individual plates. Top with the turkey burgers. Spoon the chilled cucumber salad over the burgers and serve.

....

Technique Tip: For very thin and uniform
cucumber slices, use a mandolin.

....

Mini Meatloaves
with Chunky Tomato-Basil Sauce

Serves 4 — **Nut-free**

Who said meatloaf had to be smothered in sugary ketchup to be delicious? In this recipe, classic meatloaf is enriched with sautéed vegetables and portioned into four individual loaves for quick cooking. The sauce, free of corn syrup and other preservatives, kicks ketchup to the curb with the flavorful additions of garlic, crushed red pepper flakes, and fresh herbs.

FOR THE MEATLOAVES:

1 tablespoon extra-virgin olive oil

2 medium carrots, peeled and shredded

1 medium celery stalk, peeled and finely chopped

½ medium yellow onion, finely chopped

2 garlic cloves, finely chopped

1 tablespoon tomato paste

1 teaspoon dried oregano

1 cup gluten-free crispy rice cereal, unsweetened or very lightly sweetened

1 pound lean, grass-fed ground beef

1 large egg

½ teaspoon sea salt

FOR THE SAUCE:

1 tablespoon extra-virgin olive oil

2 garlic cloves, finely chopped

¼ teaspoon crushed red pepper flakes

4 cups chopped tomatoes

Sea salt and black pepper, to taste

¼ cup fresh basil, chopped or torn

2 tablespoons finely chopped flat-leaf parsley

Preheat the oven to 425°F. Line a rimmed baking sheet with parchment paper.

Make the meatloaves: heat the olive oil in a medium skillet set over medium heat. Add the carrots, celery, and onion. Cook, stirring often, for 3-5 minutes or until the vegetables are soft. Stir in the garlic, tomato paste, and dried oregano. Cook for 1 minute or until fragrant. Remove from heat and transfer to large mixing bowl to cool.

Using a rolling pin or the bottom of a glass, lightly crush the rice cereal to form coarse crumbs. Add to the bowl with the sautéed vegetables. When vegetable mixture has cooled, add the ground beef, egg, and sea salt. Use your hands to work the ingredients into a cohesive mass. Form into 4 oval-shaped loaves about 5 inches long and 1½-inches thick. Arrange on the parchment-lined baking sheet. Bake the mini meatloaves for 30-35 minutes until cooked through. Rest for 5 minutes before serving.

While the loaves bake, make the sauce: heat the olive oil in a medium pot over medium heat. Add the garlic and red pepper flakes. Stir for 1 minute. Add the tomatoes and bring to a rapid simmer, then reduce the heat to low and cook, stirring occasionally, for 12-15 minutes or until the tomatoes have broken down into a thick and chunky sauce. Season to taste with salt and pepper. Stir in the basil and parsley.

Spoon the sauce over the meatloaves and serve, passing any remaining sauce at the table.

Taco Bowls

Serves 4 — **Egg-free, nut-free**

Don't let the long list of ingredients intimidate you here. This fun twist on tacos is a snap to make and a hit with hungry kids (or adults)! Without the drippy sauce leaking out of the taco shells, these taco bowls make for cleaner eating. Feel free to swap in cooked quinoa or millet for the rice.

1 ¼ cups long grain brown rice

2 ½ cups water

1 tablespoon extra-virgin olive oil

1 pound lean, grass-fed ground beef

½ medium yellow onion, chopped

1 medium jalapeno pepper, seeded and finely chopped (optional)

4 garlic cloves, finely chopped

1 tablespoon tomato paste

1 teaspoon ground cumin

1 teaspoon chili powder

½ teaspoon dried oregano

1 (8-ounce) can tomato sauce

2 tablespoons water

1 tablespoon honey

Sea salt and black pepper, to taste

OPTIONAL TOPPINGS:

Shredded carrots

Thinly sliced green cabbage

Chopped Roma tomatoes

Chopped cilantro or flat-leaf parsley

Diced avocado

Chopped scallions

Bring the rice and water to boil in a medium pot over high heat. Reduce the heat to low, cover, and cook until the water is absorbed and the rice is fluffy, 35-45 minutes.

Meanwhile, heat the olive oil over medium-high heat in a large skillet. Add the beef and cook until browned, crumbling up with a wooden utensil, 6-8 minutes. Reduce the heat to medium and add the onion and jalapeno. Cook, stirring occasionally, until the onion is soft and translucent, about 5 minutes. Add the garlic, tomato paste, cumin, chili powder, and oregano and stir for 1 minute. Add the tomato sauce, water, and honey. Cook for 2-3 minutes to heat through. Season to taste with salt and pepper.

Spoon the taco beef over bowls of the rice. Top as desired and serve.

Meatballs
with Quick-Braised Collards

Serves 4 — **Nut-free**

Sturdy greens like collards and kale beg for hot, slow cooking methods in the middle of winter when I don't feel like eating a cold salad. Most braised collard recipes call for simmering the greens for nearly an hour with a hefty dose of bacon and onions. To preserve the integrity of the vegetable—its flavor, color, and texture—I prefer to cook my greens briefly and with just a few simple seasonings.

1 pound lean, grass-fed ground beef

1 large egg

⅓ cup quinoa flakes

¼ cup finely chopped flat-leaf parsley

1 teaspoon Italian seasoning or all-purpose herb seasoning

½ teaspoon granulated garlic powder

¼ teaspoon sea salt (plus more to taste)

1 tablespoon extra-virgin olive oil

½ medium yellow onion, chopped

2 garlic cloves, finely chopped

2 – 3 bunches (1½ - 2 pounds) collard greens, stems removed and discarded, leaves thinly sliced

1 cup low-sodium chicken broth

1 tablespoon balsamic vinegar

1 teaspoon finely grated lemon zest

Preheat the oven to 375°F. Line a rimmed baking sheet with parchment paper.

In a medium bowl, mix together the beef, egg, quinoa flakes, parsley, Italian seasoning, garlic power, and ¼ teaspoon sea salt using your hands. Form the mixture into 12 meatballs of equal size and arrange them on the prepared baking sheet. Bake for 22-25 minutes until cooked through.

While the meatballs bake, prepare the collards: heat the olive oil in a large skillet or sauté pan over medium heat. Add the onion and cook, stirring occasionally, for about 5 minutes. Add the garlic and stir for 1 minute. Add the collard greens a few handfuls at a time, tossing after each addition to wilt them down so they all fit in the pan. When all of the greens are in the pan, add the broth and bring to a rapid simmer. Cover, reduce the heat to low, and simmer for 10-12 minutes until the greens are just tender. Stir in the vinegar and lemon zest. Season to taste with salt and pepper and remove the pan from the heat.

Arrange the cooked meatballs over the braised greens and serve.

....

Ingredient Tip: Find quinoa flakes in the cereal aisle of your grocery store or natural foods market near the oatmeal. They are also available in the bulk bins of some stores.

....

Parsnip-Topped Skillet Pie

Serves 4 — **Vegan**

Although a bit more labor-intensive than most of the recipes in this book, I couldn't leave out one of my favorite vegan skillet suppers. A plant-based riff on shepherd's pie, my version is chock-full of garden goodness. The parsnips lend a unique, woodsy edge to the topping, while the combination of mushrooms and beans gives the filling bulk and substance. Skillet pies invite you to incorporate whatever fresh produce you have on hand, so feel free to add in anything that's lurking in your crisper drawer.

FOR THE FILLING:

2 tablespoons extra-virgin olive oil

2 large carrots, peeled and chopped small

1 large yellow onion, peeled and chopped small

6 ounces green beans, trimmed and cut into 1/3-inch pieces

4 ounces cremini mushrooms, thinly sliced

4 garlic cloves, finely chopped

2 tablespoons tomato paste

1 tablespoon brown rice flour

1 teaspoon dried basil

1 teaspoon paprika

1 teaspoon ground cumin

1 (15-ounce) can pinto beans, rinsed and drained

1 cup water

Sea salt and black pepper, to taste

FOR THE TOPPING:

1 pound russet potatoes, peeled and cut into 1-inch chunks (about 2 large potatoes)

¾ pound parsnips, peeled and cut into 1-inch chunks (about 7 small to medium parsnips)

¼ cup canned coconut milk (full fat)

2 tablespoons extra-virgin olive oil

Sea salt, to taste

First, make the filling: heat the olive oil over medium-high heat in a large oven-safe skillet. Add the carrots, onion, green beans, and mushrooms. Cook, stirring occasionally, for 8-10 minutes. Add the garlic, tomato paste, flour, basil, paprika, and cumin; stir for 1 minute. Stir in the pinto beans and water. Cook until the liquid in the pan creates a thickly bubbling sauce, about 2 minutes. Remove from heat, season to taste with salt and pepper, and set aside.

Preheat the oven to 350°F. Make the topping: in a large pot, cover the potatoes and parsnips with cold water. Bring to a boil over high heat. Reduce the heat to medium-high and continue boiling until the vegetables are tender, 12-15 minutes. Drain well and return to the hot pot. Add the coconut milk and olive oil. Mash the potatoes and parsnips with a potato masher until smooth. Season to taste with salt.

Spread the potato-parsnip mash on top of the filling in the skillet. Loosely tent the skillet with a piece of parchment paper. Bake for about 20 minutes until hot throughout. Serve.

Chickpea & Mushroom Ragout with Wild Rice

Serves 4 — **Vegan**

Chickpeas are one of my favorite sources of vegetarian protein. In addition to delivering minerals and fiber, the bean's firm texture holds up well to cooking, making chickpeas an ideal choice for recipes like this hearty ragout. If you don't have rice on hand, serve the ragout over a bed of braised collard greens (page 184) or kale.

½ **cup wild rice**

½ **cup long grain brown rice**

2 cups water

1 ounce dried porcini or portabella mushrooms

1 tablespoon extra-virgin olive oil

½ **medium yellow onion, finely chopped**

2 medium celery stalks, peeled and finely chopped

2 garlic cloves, finely chopped

2 tablespoons finely chopped fresh thyme

1 tablespoon tomato paste

1 (25-ounce) can chickpeas, rinsed and drained

2 tablespoons finely chopped flat-leaf parsley

1 tablespoon balsamic vinegar

Sea salt and black pepper, to taste

¼ **cup sliced almonds, toasted (optional)**

Bring the wild rice, brown rice, and water to a boil in a medium pot over high heat. Reduce the heat to low, cover, and simmer until water is absorbed and the rice is fluffy, 35-45 minutes.

Meanwhile, place the mushrooms in a small pot and cover with several cups of water. Bring to a boil over high heat, then reduce the heat to low and simmer for 8-10 minutes to rehydrate the mushrooms. Drain, reserving ½ cup liquid, and roughly chop.

Heat the olive oil in a large skillet over medium heat. Add the onion and celery. Cook for 5 minutes until the onion is soft and translucent. Add the garlic, thyme, and tomato paste. Stir for 1 minute. Add the chickpeas, parsley, vinegar, chopped mushrooms, and reserved mushroom liquid. Cook for 3-5 minutes to heat everything through and combine the flavors. Season to taste with salt and pepper.

Serve the ragout over the rice. Garnish with the almonds, if using.

....

Technique Tip: See page 231 for a
guide to toasting nuts.

....

....

The Mighty Mushroom

Looking to beef up the flavor of your vegetarian recipes? Add some 'shrooms! With their chewy texture and earthy flavor, mushrooms lend a meat-like quality to soups, stews, ragouts, burgers, and more that can't be beat. Skip the meat substitutes available in many stores these days, which are almost always a storehouse of preservatives, gluten, and refined sugar. The next time you want to add a little oomph to a meatless meal, reach for mushrooms instead.

....

Black Bean & Quinoa Patties

Serves 4 — **Vegan, nut-free**

Bean patties are a blank slate, adapting easily to a wide variety of flavor pairings. Escape to India with curry powder and lentils. Go Greek with chickpeas, red onions, and garlic. Or, as presented in this delicious variation, head South-of-the-Border with cilantro, cumin, and chili powder. Serve the patties with a dollop of the Fiesta Guacamole on page 100.

1 (15-ounce) can black beans, rinsed and drained

1 ¼ cups cooked quinoa, cooled to room temperature or refrigerated

2 garlic cloves

2 medium scallions, roughly chopped (white and green parts)

¼ cup fresh cilantro or flat-leaf parsley

1 tablespoon tomato paste

1 tablespoon brown rice flour or sorghum flour

1½ teaspoons ground cumin

¾ teaspoon chili powder

½ teaspoon sea salt

1 tablespoon extra-virgin olive oil

Large lettuce leaves

OPTIONAL TOPPINGS:

Salsa

Shredded carrots

Thinly sliced red onions

In a food processor fitted with the steel blade, combine the black beans, quinoa, garlic, scallions, cilantro, tomato paste, flour, cumin, chili powder, and sea salt. Process until just combined, 15-20 seconds.

Form the mixture into four ½-inch thick patties of equal size. Arrange the patties on a parchment-lined plate and freeze, uncovered, for 20-30 minutes.

Heat the olive oil in a large skillet over medium heat. Add the patties and cook for about 4 minutes per side. Arrange each patty on a lettuce leaf, top as desired, and serve.

....

Technique Tip: Make sure your quinoa is completely cooled before making these patties. They actually hold their shape best if the quinoa has been refrigerated for several hours prior to using. If you cook the quinoa in advance, the patties will come together quickly.

....

....

Quinoa: The Pseudo Grain

Although it cooks up and tastes like a grain, quinoa (pronounced KEEN-wah) is actually a seed and therefore considered a "pseudo grain." Packed with protein, vitamins, and minerals, this little powerhouse offers all nine essential amino acids (the building blocks of protein and muscle), making it a source of complete protein and an excellent addition to vegetarian and vegan diets.
To make matters even better, quinoa cooks up in less than half the time of brown rice.

....

Vegan Sloppy Joe Bowls

Serves 4 — **Vegan, nut-free**

Beans and rice are one of the most basic and versatile blank canvases of the culinary world. This variation bumps up the protein of the dish by swapping in quinoa for the rice. I love a good "Meatless Monday" supper, and this one has quickly become a favorite.

1 tablespoon extra-virgin olive oil

½ medium yellow onion, chopped small

2 garlic cloves, finely chopped

1 tablespoon tomato paste

1 teaspoon dried basil

½ teaspoon ground cumin

1 (15-ounce) can pinto beans, rinsed and drained

1 (15-ounce) can black beans, rinsed and drained

1 (8-ounce) can tomato sauce

½ cup fresh or frozen corn kernels (no need to thaw)

⅓ cup water

1 tablespoon agave nectar or dark maple syrup

1 tablespoon apple cider vinegar

2 teaspoons blackstrap molasses

Sea salt and black pepper, to taste

FOR SERVING:

Cooked quinoa, warm

Thinly sliced scallions or red onion

Sprouts or microgreens

Shredded lettuce

In a large sauté pan or Dutch oven, heat the olive oil over medium heat. Add the onion and cook, stirring occasionally, until soft and translucent, about 5 minutes. Add the garlic, tomato paste, basil, and cumin; stir for 1 minute.

Add half of the pinto and black beans. Squash the beans using a potato masher to achieve a chunky texture. Stir in the remaining beans, tomato sauce, corn, water, agave nectar, vinegar, and molasses. Bring to a rapid simmer, then reduce the heat to low and simmer for about 10 minutes to blend the flavors. Season to taste with salt and pepper.

Serve the bean mixture over bowls of quinoa topped with the scallions, sprouts, and shredded lettuce.

Satisfying Sweets & Treats

Exploring a range of whole grain flours and natural sweeteners is something I always find inspiring. Not only do ingredients like maple syrup, honey, coconut sugar, and fruit purees lend sweetness to desserts and treats, but they also contribute to the overall depth of flavor.

Fresh, seasonal fruit lays the foundation for many of my dessert recipes. One of my personal pet peeves is biting into a cake or cookie only to have the intense, sugary sweetness offend my taste buds. As with my baked goods, using fewer sweeteners in my desserts allows the flavors of the flours, fruits, and spices to take center stage.

Pure eating allows plenty of room for enjoying the occasional sweet or treat, but remember the vital concept of moderation! Although my desserts are healthier than many traditional recipes, they're still desserts. Savoring them every once in a while instead of every other meal leads to better health and a deeper appreciation for the sweet side of pure living.

For the recipes in this section that are baked, refer to pages 75-78 of the Wholesome Baked Goods section for important tips regarding gluten-free, dairy-free baking.

Kitchen Sink Health Cookies

Makes 12-14 cookies — **Vegan**

When I first began cooking healthfully with natural ingredients, these cookies were my staple treat. I came to call them by this name because I throw in everything but the kitchen sink. They have a soft texture and fruity flavor.

2 medium very ripe bananas, mashed well (about a heaping ½ cup)

½ cup unsweetened applesauce

¼ cup extra-virgin olive oil

2 tablespoons dark maple syrup

1 cup quinoa flakes

¼ cup (29 grams) coconut flour

1 teaspoon baking powder

1 teaspoon ground cinnamon

¼ teaspoon salt

½ cup chopped walnuts

¼ cup raisins

¼ cup dairy-free dark chocolate chips

¼ cup sunflower seeds

Preheat the oven to 350°F. Line 2 baking sheets with parchment paper.

In a medium bowl, whisk together the mashed bananas, applesauce, olive oil, and maple syrup. In a large bowl, whisk together the quinoa flakes, coconut flour, baking powder, cinnamon, and salt. Stir the wet ingredients into the dry until thoroughly combined. Stir in the walnuts, raisins, chocolate chips, and sunflower seeds.

Drop the dough onto the parchment-lined baking sheets, using about 2 tablespoons of dough per cookie. Flatten the cookies to ½-inch thick using your fingertips. Bake for about 15 minutes or until the cookies are firm to the touch and lightly browned.

Cool completely before serving. Store in an airtight container in the refrigerator.

....

Ingredient Note: Dark chocolate chips contain refined sugar.
I use them on rare occasions in my baking as a special treat,
always choosing organic. If you would prefer to make these
cookies completely free of refined sugar, double the raisins
or add in dried currants.

....

Thick & Chewy
Peanut Butter Cookies

Makes 22-24 cookies — **Vegan**

I know everyone seems to think that their grandmother made the best peanut butter cookies, but trust me on this one; my grandma's really were the very best! Soft and cakey, her cookies never lasted long once my dad and I found them waiting for us in the freezer. This recipe is a nod to Grandma's peanut butter cookies. While nothing will ever match up to her homemade baked goods, I must say that these cookies are a darn good variation on a classic cookie— made entirely free of gluten, dairy, and sugar.

½ cup (packed) pitted Medjool dates

¼ cup hot water

¼ cup virgin coconut oil or grapeseed oil

¼ cup dark maple syrup or agave nectar

1 cup creamy, unsweetened peanut butter

3 tablespoons ground flaxseed, preferably golden

1 cup gluten-free rolled oats

¼ cup (34 grams) brown rice flour

¼ cup (27 grams) arrowroot starch

1 teaspoon baking soda

Pinch of sea salt

Preheat the oven to 350°F. Line 2 rimmed baking sheets with parchment paper. In a small bowl, soak the dates in the hot water for 5-10 minutes.

Transfer the soaked dates (and the water) to a blender. Add the coconut oil and maple syrup. Blend on high until very smooth. Scrape the mixture into the bowl of a stand mixer fitted with the paddle attachment. (If you do not have a stand mixer, transfer the mixture to a large bowl and proceed using a handheld electric mixer.)

Add the peanut butter and flaxseed to the bowl and beat on medium speed until combined. Add the remaining ingredients and beat until a thick dough forms.

Roll the dough into 1½-inch balls. Arrange the balls on the lined baking sheets. Using the bottom of a small glass, gently flatten each ball to about 1/3-inch thick. Bake the cookies for 10-12 minutes until brown around the edges. Cool cookies completely on sheets before serving or storing. The cookies will be soft to the touch, but will firm up as they cool. Store in an airtight container.

Ingredient Note: You can use either unsalted or salted peanut butter here. If you use salted, you may want to omit the pinch of sea salt.

Chocolate-Peanut Butter Sandwich Variation:
Sandwich a teaspoon or two of Luscious Chocolate Pudding (page 221) between two cookies for a decadent treat.

Lemon Bars
with Oatmeal-Coconut Crust

Makes 16 bars

Most lemon bars are tooth-achingly sweet and guaranteed to spike your blood sugar. These zesty bars offer plenty of lemon flavor and sweetness without all the refined sugar.

FOR THE CRUST:

- **1 cup gluten-free rolled oats**
- **½ cup finely shredded unsweetened coconut**
- **¼ teaspoon baking soda**
- **¼ teaspoon sea salt**
- **2 tablespoons unsweetened applesauce**
- **2 tablespoons agave nectar**

FOR THE LEMON LAYER:

- **⅓ cup fresh lemon juice**
- **¼ cup virgin coconut oil, melted and cooled (plus more for greasing the pan)**
- **¼ cup agave nectar**
- **3 large eggs**
- **1 tablespoon finely grated lemon zest**
- **½ cup finely shredded unsweetened coconut**

Preheat the oven to 350°F. Lightly grease an 8x8-inch glass or ceramic baking dish with coconut oil. Set aside.

Make the crust: in a food processor fitted with the steel blade, process the oats, coconut, baking soda, and salt to form a coarse meal. Add the applesauce and agave nectar. Process until a dough forms. Press the dough firmly and evenly into the bottom of the greased baking dish. Bake for about 12 minutes until lightly golden.

Make the lemon layer: whisk together the lemon juice, coconut oil, agave nectar, and eggs in a medium bowl. Pour the lemon mixture over the hot oatmeal crust and return to the oven to bake for 15-18 minutes, or until golden brown around the edges. Remove from the oven and sprinkle with the shredded coconut.

Cool completely at room temperature, then refrigerate for at least 2 hours before cutting into bars and serving. Store leftover bars in an airtight container in the refrigerator.

....

Ingredient Tip: Finely shredded coconut may also be labeled "flaked" or "ground" coconut. Either one will work. Just make sure it is unsweetened.

....

....

Sweets in a Snap

Fruit is nature's perfect dessert, so try these fruity quick fixes the next time you have a sweet tooth:

✓ Pitted dates stuffed with almonds or pecans

✓ Dried apricots or figs

✓ Bananas cut into chunks, dipped in almond butter, and topped with raisins

✓ Seasonal fruit topped with a few nuts or seeds and drizzled with coconut milk

✓ Unsweetened applesauce topped with shredded coconut and cinnamon

....

Peanut Butter Freezer Treats

Makes about 18 balls — **Vegan**

Imagine a cross between peanut butter ice cream, chocolate fudge, caramel candies, and date balls—and you get these. I'm officially addicted. And I'm pretty sure you will be too.

½ cup creamy, unsweetened peanut butter

¼ cup unsweetened applesauce

3 tablespoons coconut sugar

2 tablespoons virgin coconut oil, melted

1 tablespoon dark maple syrup

Pinch of sea salt

½ cup quinoa flakes

¼ cup (24 grams) blanched almond flour

2 tablespoons (15 grams) coconut flour

2 tablespoons raw sunflower seeds

2 tablespoons dairy-free dark chocolate chips (optional)

2 tablespoons raisins

Chopped nuts, for rolling (optional)

In a large mixing bowl, combine the peanut butter, applesauce, coconut sugar, coconut oil, maple syrup, and salt. Add the quinoa flakes, almond flour, and coconut flour and mix well to combine. Stir in the sunflower seeds, chocolate chips (if using), and raisins.

Form the dough into small balls about 1 – 1½-inches in diameter. Roll the balls in the nuts, if using, and freeze in an even layer on a plate until firm, about 1 hour. Transfer the balls to an airtight container and keep frozen until ready to serve. Thaw for 2-3 minutes at room temperature before serving.

Ingredient Note: Omit the sea salt if you are using salted peanut butter. If you are allergic to peanuts, swap in almond, cashew, or sunflower seed butter. For a completely refined sugar-free treat, omit the chocolate chips.

Dark Chocolate Brownie Balls

Makes about 25 balls — **Vegan**

These balls were among the first treats I created after going gluten-free. While not a spitting image of brownies, they are certainly a tasty spin-off that got me through many a candy craving those first few months of living without gluten.

1 ½ cups raw walnuts

1 medium vanilla bean

2/3 cup (packed) pitted Medjool dates

½ cup (packed) raisins

2 teaspoons (packed) finely grated orange zest

¼ cup unsweetened cocoa powder

Pinch of sea salt

In a food processor fitted with the steel blade, process the walnuts until finely ground, about 25 seconds.

Using a sharp knife, split the vanilla bean in half lengthwise. Use the side of the knife to scrape the tiny seeds out of the pod. Add them to the food processor along the remaining ingredients. Process until the ingredients are thoroughly incorporated and the dough holds together when pinched between your fingers, about 30 seconds.

Roll the dough into small balls. Refrigerate in an airtight container for up to 3 days.

Two-Bite Raspberry Lemon Tartlets

Makes 16-18 — **Vegan**

These raw-inspired tartlets are as beautiful to look at as they are to eat. The bright green avocado cream offers tang that's perfectly balanced by the sweetness of the walnut-date crust.

1 medium ripe avocado, halved and pitted

2 tablespoons fresh lemon juice

2 tablespoons agave nectar

2 tablespoons virgin coconut oil, melted and cooled

1 teaspoon (packed) finely grated lemon zest

1½ cups raw walnuts

¾ cup (packed) pitted Medjool dates

16-18 fresh raspberries

In food processor fitted with the steel blade, process the avocado, lemon juice, agave nectar, coconut oil, and lemon zest until smooth and creamy, stopping several times to scrape down the sides of the bowl with a rubber spatula. Transfer the avocado cream to a piping bag fitted with a star tip and freeze until thoroughly chilled but still malleable, 1½ - 2 hours.

Clean out the food processor and add the walnuts. Process the walnuts until finely ground. Add the dates and process until the mixture holds together when pinched between your fingers. If the mixture feels dry and will not hold together, pulse in ½ teaspoon of water at a time to achieve the right consistency. Form the mixture into a flat disk and wrap in waxed paper or plastic wrap. Freeze for 45-60 minutes.

Roll the walnut dough into balls roughly 1 – 1½ inches in diameter. Flatten each ball to form small disks about 1/3-inch thick. Arrange them on a platter and pipe the avocado cream on top of each disk. Top with the raspberries and serve. (The tarts can be refrigerated at this point for up to 2 hours.)

....

Technique Tip: If you don't have a piping bag, use a
plastic food storage bag instead, snipping off one of the corners
for a makeshift piping bag.

....

Old Fashioned Fruit Crisp

Serves 4 to 6 — **Vegan**

This is my stand-by summer dessert. Everyone loves it and it's so easy you could probably make it blindfolded. (But I wouldn't advise it.) Using applesauce in the topping adds moisture and chewy texture, allowing for a cut-back on the fat.

5 cups sliced fresh fruit, such as peaches, pears, plums, apples, or strawberries

¼ cup (27 grams) plus 2 tablespoons (14 grams) arrowroot starch, divided

2 tablespoons agave nectar

1 tablespoon fresh lemon juice

1 cup gluten-free rolled oats

⅓ cup chopped pecans (optional)

⅓ cup coconut sugar

¼ cup (32 grams) millet flour

1 teaspoon ground cinnamon

Pinch of sea salt

¼ cup virgin coconut oil, melted

2 tablespoons unsweetened applesauce

Preheat the oven to 350°F. In a large mixing bowl, toss the fruit with 2 tablespoons of the arrowroot starch, agave nectar, and lemon juice. Transfer to an 8x8-inch baking dish or 9-inch deep dish pie plate.

In a medium bowl, mix together the remaining ¼ cup arrowroot starch, oats, pecans (if using), coconut sugar, millet flour, cinnamon, and salt. Add the coconut oil and applesauce. Mix to form a crumbly topping.

Scatter the topping over the fruit. Bake for 35-40 minutes until the juices are bubbly. Cool for at least 30 minutes before serving.

Berry Bowls
with Fudgy Pecan Crumble

Serves 4 — **Egg-free**

As is true with most fruit-based desserts, use the freshest and most seasonal berries you can find. Your taste buds will thank you. If berries are not in season, chopped peaches, nectarines, or pitted cherries make a mouthwatering substitute.

**2 cups mixed fresh berries such as strawberries (halved if large),
    blueberries, raspberries, or blackberries**

1 tablespoon fresh lemon juice

1 tablespoon honey

½ teaspoon ground cinnamon

¾ cup raw pecans

½ cup (packed) pitted Medjool dates

2 tablespoons unsweetened cocoa powder

1 teaspoon finely grated orange zest, optional

Pinch of sea salt

Mint leaves, for garnish

In a medium mixing bowl, toss the berries with the lemon juice, honey, and cinnamon. Refrigerate for at least 30 minutes or up to 2 hours.

In a food processor fitted with the steel blade, process the pecans until finely ground. Add the dates and cocoa powder. Process for 15-20 seconds until incorporated. Add the orange zest and salt. Process until the mixture holds together when pinched between two fingers.

To serve, divide the berries among 4 serving bowls. Crumble the date and pecan mixture over the top of the berries. Garnish with the mint and serve.

....

Retraining Your Taste Buds

Cooking without sugar may leave you feeling like
the naturally sweetened goodies you're making aren't very sweet.
Don't worry. It usually takes a good three to six months—
sometimes longer—to whip your taste buds back into shape
and begin noticing the varying levels of sweetness between
naturally sweetened and sugary treats. Stick with it!

....

Maple Pecan Tart

Serves 6 to 8

This decadent tart makes an appearance on my table every holiday season. It's rich and indulgent without being overly sweet. Adding teff flour to the crust provides structure and a bit of earthy, rustic flavor.

FOR THE CRUST:

¾ cup (102 grams) teff flour

½ cup (54 grams) arrowroot starch

½ cup raw pecans

1 tablespoon coconut sugar

1 teaspoon ground cinnamon

½ teaspoon sea salt

¼ cup virgin coconut oil, room temperature (not melted)

3 tablespoons water

FOR THE FILLING:

1 cup raw pecans

2 large eggs

2 large egg whites

½ cup dark maple syrup

2 tablespoons coconut sugar

1 tablespoon apple cider vinegar

2 teaspoons vanilla extract

Pinch of sea salt

Preheat the oven to 350°F. Make the crust: in a food processor fitted with the steel blade, combine the teff flour, arrowroot starch, pecans, coconut sugar, cinnamon, and salt. Process until the pecans are finely ground. Add the coconut oil and process until the mixture looks like damp sand. Add the water and process until incorporated into the dry ingredients and the mixture holds together when pinched with two fingers, 20-30 seconds.

Press the dough firmly and evenly into the bottom and up the sides of a 9-inch tart pan with a removable bottom. Place the tart pan on a rimmed baking sheet and bake for 10-12 minutes. Remove from the oven and cool the crust for at least 15 minutes before filling.

While the crust cools, make the filling: finely chop ¼ cup of the pecans. Whisk the chopped pecans with the eggs, egg whites, maple syrup, coconut sugar, vinegar, vanilla, and salt in a medium mixing bowl until thoroughly combined. Pour into the tart shell. Scatter the remaining ¾ cup pecans over the top of the filling.

Bake the tart for 23-25 minutes until the filling is puffed and golden brown. Cool to room temperature before serving. Store leftovers in an airtight container in the refrigerator.

....

Tips for Healthy Holidays

✓ Load up on the veggie platter. Fresh cut vegetables are naturally gluten- and dairy-free, not to mention the healthiest option on most holiday buffets.

✓ Bring your own dish to share. You'll know what's in it and ensure that you have something safe to eat at the gathering.

✓ Stay hydrated. If you fall off the pure living wagon around the holidays and splurge on a few too many sweets, drinking lots of water will help your body detoxify more efficiently.

✓ Prioritize sleep! People are generally more stressed and anxious during the holiday season, which is all the more reason to restore and recharge with a good night's rest.

....

Brownie-Crusted Berry Pizza

Serves 6 to 8

When I was in my early teens, I was obsessed with pies and tarts, spending nearly every weekend trying a new recipe. I went on to make and sell pies to the neighbors around the holidays. Although I don't eat gluten or dairy anymore, I can still indulge my love of tart-making with scrumptious recipes like this one.

¼ cup virgin coconut oil (plus more for greasing the pan)

2 ounces unsweetened chocolate, roughly chopped

¼ cup coconut sugar

1 large egg, lightly beaten

¼ cup (27 grams) arrowroot starch

½ teaspoon baking powder

¼ teaspoon sea salt

1 cup raw cashews, covered with water and soaked at room temperature for 3-4 hours

2 tablespoons agave nectar

1 tablespoon water

1 medium vanilla bean

1½ - 2 cups blueberries, raspberries, sliced strawberries, or a combination

Preheat the oven to 325°F. Lightly oil the bottom of a 9-inch spring form pan with coconut oil.

In a medium pot over low heat, melt the coconut oil and chocolate until smooth, whisking constantly. Remove from heat and whisk in the coconut sugar. Transfer to a medium mixing bowl and cool for 5 minutes. Whisk in the egg, arrowroot starch, baking powder, and salt. Transfer the batter to the greased pan. Spread it out into an even layer using a rubber spatula. It will be thick and oily, so take your time to ensure even distribution without holes. Bake the crust for about 10 minutes or until dry to the touch and slightly puffed.

While the crust bakes, make the cashew topping: drain the cashews well and add them to a high-speed blender. Add the agave nectar, 1 tablespoon water, and the whole vanilla bean. Blend on high until smooth and creamy, stopping several times to scrape down the sides of the blender with a spoon or rubber spatula.

Once the crust has cooled, unmold it from the pan and place it on a serving platter. Spread the cashew cream evenly over the cooled crust. Arrange the berries on top in desired pattern. Serve right away or refrigerate, covered, for up to 1 hour.

Technique Tip: If you don't have a high-speed blender, you can still make the cashew cream using a regular blender or food processor. Soak the cashews for 8 hours and replace the vanilla bean with 1 teaspoon of vanilla extract. You may need to add additional water as you blend to achieve a smooth consistency. The result will not be quite as smooth as cream made with a high-speed blender, but it will still taste delicious.

Banana Coconut Cupcakes
with Fudgy Chocolate Frosting

Makes 12

Moist with a tender crumb and mouthwatering banana flavor, these nutritious yet indulgent cupcakes top my list of favorite desserts in this book. Get fancy and garnish them with fresh banana slices just before serving if you'd like.

FOR THE FROSTING:

½ cup (packed) pitted Medjool dates

½ medium ripe avocado, roughly mashed

¼ cup creamy roasted cashew butter

3 tablespoons unsweetened cocoa powder

1 tablespoon agave nectar

FOR THE CUPCAKES:

½ cup (58 grams) coconut flour

2 tablespoons (14 grams) arrowroot starch

½ teaspoon baking soda

Pinch of sea salt

4 large eggs

½ cup agave nectar

2 medium very ripe bananas, mashed

Make the frosting: cover the dates with hot water in a small bowl and soak for 10 minutes. Drain well, reserving 1 tablespoon of the soaking liquid, and place both the dates and reserved liquid in the bowl of a food processor fitted with the steel blade. Add the mashed avocado and cashew butter. Process until smooth. Add the cocoa powder and agave nectar. Process until thick and fudgy, stopping once or twice to scrape down the sides of the bowl with a rubber spatula. Refrigerate the frosting until ready to use.

Makes the cupcakes: preheat the oven to 350°F. Line 12 cups of a standard muffin pan with paper liners. In a large bowl, whisk together the coconut flour, arrowroot starch, baking soda, and salt. In a medium bowl, whisk together the eggs, agave nectar, and mashed bananas. Stir the wet ingredients into the dry until thoroughly combined.

Divide the batter evenly among the lined muffin cups. Bake for 20-25 minutes until golden brown and a toothpick inserted into the center of a cupcake comes out clean. Cool the cupcakes completely in the pan before frosting.

Lemon Blueberry Cornmeal Cake

Serves 12

Cornmeal lends texture and a bit of crunch to this fruity cake. It could actually pass for a breakfast cake that would pair perfectly with a warm cup of coffee or tea.

1 cup (104 grams) plus 2 tablespoons (13 grams) sorghum flour

½ cup (70 grams) medium-grind gluten-free cornmeal

2 tablespoons ground flaxseed

2 teaspoons baking powder

¼ teaspoon sea salt

½ cup extra-virgin olive oil (plus more for greasing the pan)

½ cup agave nectar

¼ cup unsweetened almond or rice milk

2 large eggs

1 tablespoon fresh lemon juice

1 tablespoon finely grated lemon zest

1 heaping cup fresh blueberries

Preheat the oven to 350°F. Lightly oil an 8x8-inch baking dish with olive oil.

In a large bowl, whisk together the sorghum flour, cornmeal, flaxseed, baking powder, and salt. In a separate bowl, whisk together the olive oil, agave nectar, almond milk, eggs, lemon juice, and lemon zest. Pour the wet ingredients into the dry and stir to combine. Fold in the blueberries. Transfer the batter to the oiled baking dish.

Bake for 30-35 minutes or until golden brown and a toothpick inserted into the center of the cake comes out clean. Cool cake completely before cutting into squares and serving.

Swap It: Try chopped peaches or strawberries instead of the blueberries.

Death by Chocolate Cake

Serves 8

Every cookbook needs a good chocolate cake recipe, and this one is everything a chocolate cake should be: moist, dense, deeply chocolate flavored, and entirely indulgent.

½ **cup unsweetened almond milk**

2 **tablespoons ground chia seeds**

¼ **cup virgin coconut oil (plus more for greasing the pan)**

1 **ounce unsweetened chocolate, roughly chopped**

½ **cup coconut sugar**

2 **large eggs**

½ **cup unsweetened applesauce**

½ **cup (68 grams) teff flour**

¼ **cup plus 2 tablespoons unsweetened cocoa powder**

1 **teaspoon baking powder**

¼ **teaspoon baking soda**

Pinch of sea salt

Luscious Chocolate Pudding (page 221), for frosting

Preheat the oven to 350°F. Line the bottom of an 8-inch cake pan with a circle of parchment paper. Lightly oil the parchment and sides of the pan with coconut oil.

Bring the almond milk to a simmer in a small pot. Transfer to a heat-safe bowl and vigorously whisk in the chia seeds to form a slurry. Set aside to thicken.

Melt the coconut oil and chocolate in a small pot over very low heat until smooth. Transfer to the bowl of a stand mixer fitted with the paddle attachment. (If you don't have a stand mixer, proceed with the recipe using a large bowl and a handheld electric mixer.) With the mixer on medium, gradually add the coconut sugar, beating for about 2 minutes total. Scrape down the sides of the bowl with a rubber spatula and add the chia seed mixture, eggs, and applesauce. Beat to combine. Add the teff flour, cocoa powder, baking powder, baking soda, and salt. Beat until thoroughly combined.

Transfer the batter to the prepared pan. Bake for 25-30 minutes until a toothpick inserted into the center of the cake comes out clean. Cool the cake completely in the pan before removing, frosting, and serving.

....

Tip: One recipe of Luscious Chocolate Pudding
will yield more frosting than you need for this cake.
Save the extra for snacking. Also, keep the
pudding chilled until you are ready to frost, as
cold pudding spreads a bit more easily.

....

Apple Spice Cake
with "Caramel" Frosting

Serves 8 to 10

The aroma of a house filled with the fragrance of a baking cake is just about as good as it gets. This one bursts with autumnal spices, sweet apples, and a killer "faux caramel" frosting that I'd happily eat with a spoon.

2 tablespoons boiling hot water

1 tablespoon ground flaxseed

1 cup (104 grams) sorghum flour

½ cup (67 grams) brown rice flour

½ cup (52 grams) tapioca starch

2 teaspoons baking powder

2 teaspoons ground cinnamon

1 teaspoon ground ginger

¼ teaspoon freshly grated nutmeg

½ teaspoon sea salt

¼ cup plus 2 tablespoons virgin coconut oil, melted (plus more for greasing the pan)

¼ cup plus 2 tablespoons honey

2 tablespoons molasses

1 teaspoon vanilla extract

2 large eggs

¼ cup unsweetened applesauce

1 medium Gala apple, peeled, cored, and chopped small

"Caramel" Frosting (page 220)

Preheat the oven to 350°F. Line the bottom of a 9-inch cake pan with parchment paper. Lightly oil the parchment paper and the sides of the pan with coconut oil. In a small bowl, vigorously whisk together the boiling water and ground flaxseed with a fork to form a paste. Set aside to thicken.

In a medium bowl, whisk together the sorghum flour, brown rice flour, tapioca starch, baking powder, cinnamon, ginger, nutmeg, and sea salt. In the bowl of a stand mixer fitted with the paddle attachment, beat together the coconut oil, honey, molasses, and vanilla on medium speed. (Alternatively, use a handheld electric mixer and a large bowl.) Beat in the eggs 1 at a time, then add the flaxseed slurry. Add half of the flour mixture and beat until combined. Beat in the applesauce, then the remaining flour mixture. Fold in the chopped apple.

Transfer the batter to the prepared cake pan. Bake for about 35 minutes until a toothpick inserted into the center of the cake comes out clean and the cake is deeply golden brown. Cool completely in the pan before removing, frosting, and serving.

....

Jazz It Up: Top the frosted cake with chopped pecans or sliced almonds for a crunchy garnish.

....

"Caramel" Frosting

Makes about 1 heaping cup — **Vegan**

You'd never know that this rich and creamy frosting is entirely free of refined sugar!

1 cup (packed) pitted Medjool dates

½ cup raw cashews

1 tablespoon dark maple syrup

Pinch of sea salt

Pinch of ground cinnamon

Place the dates and cashews in two separate bowls and cover each with water. Soak for 3-4 hours at room temperature.

Drain the dates well, reserving 2 tablespoons of the soaking liquid. Place the dates and reserved soaking liquid in a food processor fitted with the steel blade. Drain the cashews well and add to the processor with the dates. Add the remaining ingredients and process for 2-3 minutes until smooth and creamy, stopping several times to scrape down the sides of the bowl with a rubber spatula. Refrigerate the frosting in an airtight container until ready to use, or up to 2 days.

Luscious Chocolate Pudding

*Serves 4 to 6 — **Vegan***

Give me a bowl of this pudding and a spoon and I can do some serious damage! Thick and creamy, you'd never know that it's dairy-free and naturally sweetened. But here's the big secret: this pudding makes a fabulous frosting. Use it on the Death by Chocolate Cake on page 216 or the Banana Coconut Cupcakes on page 212.

1 cup (packed) pitted Medjool dates

3 tablespoons dark maple syrup

3 medium firm but ripe avocados, halved, pitted, and coarsely mashed

1 teaspoon finely grated orange zest

2 teaspoons vanilla extract

Pinch of sea salt

¼ cup plus 1 tablespoon unsweetened cocoa powder

OPTIONAL TOPPINGS:

Fresh berries

Slivered almonds, toasted

Cover the dates with water and soak at room temperature for 6-8 hours. Drain well, reserving 2 tablespoons of the soaking liquid. Combine the drained dates, reserved soaking liquid, and maple syrup in a food processor fitted with the steel blade. Process for about 1 minute to form a paste, stopping several times to scrape down the sides of the bowl with a rubber spatula.

Add the mashed avocados, orange zest, vanilla, and salt. Process for 1-2 minutes until the mixture is creamy and the dates are reduced to tiny flecks, stopping several times to scrape down the sides of the bowl with a rubber spatula.

Add the cocoa powder and process until thoroughly incorporated, about 1 minute, again stopping several times to scrape down the sides of the bowl. Chill the pudding before serving, if desired. Top as desired.

APPENDIX

. . . . .

Resources

Kitchen Equipment Suppliers

KitchenAid, for stand mixers and other kitchen equipment:
www.kitchenaid.com

Microplane, for handheld graters:
www.microplane.com

Sur La Table, for kitchen supplies and equipment:
www.surlatable.com

Vitamix, for professional quality high-speed blenders:
www.vitamix.com

Williams-Sonoma, for kitchen supplies and equipment:
www.williams-sonoma.com

Ingredients

Ancient Harvest, for quinoa and quinoa flakes:
www.quinoa.net

Arrowhead Mills, for organic gluten-free grains and flours:
www.arrowheadmills.com

Benefit Your Life, for blanched almond flour and other natural products:
www.benefityourlife.com

Bionaturae, for unsweetened fruit spreads and other gluten-free products: *www.bionaturae.com*

Bob's Red Mill, for gluten-free grains and flours: *www.bobsredmill.com*

Eden Organic, for organic canned foods and other natural products: *www.edenfoods.com*

Muir Glen Organic, for organic tomato products without added sugar: *www.muirglen.com*

Spectrum, for organic cooking oils: *www.spectrumorganics.com*

Sweet Tree Sustainable Sweeteners, for organic coconut (palm) sugar: *www.sweet-tree.biz*

Tinkyada, for gluten-free whole grain pastas: *www.tinkyada.com*

Tropical Traditions, for coconut oil and other natural products: *www.tropicaltraditions.com*

Vital Choice, wild and sustainable seafood and other organic products: *www.vitalchoice.com*

Wholesome Sweeteners, for organic natural sweeteners: *www.wholesomesweeteners.com*

Nutrtion & Health Resources

Local Harvest, for information about locally farmed food and tools for finding farms, farmers' markets, and community supported agriculture programs: *www.localharvest.org*

Shopper's Guide to Pesticides in Produce:
http://www.ewg.org/foodnews/summary/

Sustainable Seafood Guide:
http://www.greenamerica.org/PDF/TipSheetSafeSeafood.pdf

The World's Healthiest Foods, for information on natural foods, nutrition, and subjects related to health: *www.whfoods.org*

Recommended Reading

GLUTEN-FREE COOKBOOKS

Amsterdam, Elana. *The Gluten-Free Almond Flour Cookbook*. Berkeley: Celestial Arts, 2009.

Bronski, Kelli and Peter. *Artisanal Gluten-Free Cooking*. New York: The Experiment, 2009.

Brozyna, Kelly. *The Spunky Coconut Grain-Free Baked Goods & Desserts*. Apidae Press, 2010.

Green, Amy. *Simply Sugar and Gluten-Free: 180 Easy and Delicious Recipes You Can Make in 20 Minutes or Less*. Berkeley: Ulysses Press, 2011.

Nardone, Silvana. *Cooking for Isaiah: Gluten-Free & Dairy-Free Recipes for Easy Delicious Meals*. New York: Reader's Digest, 2010.

Segersten, Alissa and Malterre, Tom, MS CN. *The Whole Life Nutrition Cookbook, Second Edition: Whole Foods Recipes for Personal and Planetary Health*. Bellingham, Washington: Whole Life Press, 2007.

OTHER COOKBOOKS

Editors of Whole Living Magazine. *Power Foods*. New York: Clarkson Potter, 2010.

Fleming, Alisa Marie. *Go Dairy Free: The Guide and Cookbook for Milk Allergies, Lactose Intolerance, and Casein-Free Living*. Henderson, Nevada: Fleming Ink, 2008.

Katz, Rebecca. *The Cancer-Fighting Kitchen: Nourishing, Big Flavor Recipes for Cancer Treatment and Recovery*. Berkeley: Celestial Arts, 2009.

Lawson, Jane. *The Spice Bible: Essential Information and More Than 250 Recipes Using Spices, Spice Mixes, and Spice Pastes*. New York: Stewart, Tabori & Chang, 2008.

Stewart, Martha. *Martha Stewart's Dinner at Home: 52 Quick Meals to Cook for Family and Friends*. New York: Clarkson Potter, 2009.

Swanson, Heidi. *Super Natural Everyday: Well-Loved Recipes from My Natural Foods Kitchen*. Berkeley: Ten Speed Press, 2011.

OTHER BOOKS

Balch, Phyllis A. CNC. *Prescription for Nutritional Healing, Fourth Edition.* New York: Avery Trade, 2006.

Gittleman, Ann Louise. *Get the Sugar Out, Second Edition: 501 Simple Ways to Cut the Sugar Out of Any Diet.* New York: Three Rivers Press, 2008.

Lipski, Elizabeth, Ph.D., CCN. *Digestive Wellness, Third Edition.* New York: McGraw-Hill, 2005.

Murray, Michael and Pizzorno, Joseph. *The Encyclopedia of Healing Foods.* New York: Atria Books, 2005.

Pollan, Michael. *Food Rules: An Eater's Manual.* New York: Penguin Group, 2009.

Ross, Julia. *The Diet Cure.* New York: Penguin Group, 1999.

Cooking
Whole Grains

My top three go-to whole grains are brown rice, quinoa, and millet. (Quinoa is actually a seed, but it behaves like a grain in the way that it is cooked and prepared.) Below and on the page that follows are three basic recipes for cooking these grains. The cooked amount that you end up with will vary depending upon the size of the grains, how much water they absorb, and other variables. But as a general rule of thumb, one cup of dry grain cooks up to serve three to four.

Millet

This hypoallergenic grain is easy to digest and reminds me of couscous. It's mild, slightly sweet flavor pairs well with just about any main dish.

1 cup millet, rinsed and drained

2 cups water

Pinch of sea salt (optional)

Bring all of the ingredients to a boil in a medium pot over high heat. Reduce the heat to low, cover, and simmer until the water is absorbed and the millet is tender, about 25-35 minutes. Fluff up the millet with a fork before serving.

Brown Rice

Long-grain, medium-grain, and short-grain brown rice all have the same basic cooking method, so you can use them interchangeably in this recipe.

1 cup brown rice

2 cups water

Pinch of sea salt (optional)

Bring all of the ingredients to a boil in a medium pot over high heat. Reduce the heat to low, cover, and simmer until the water is absorbed and the rice is tender, about 35-45 minutes. Fluff up the rice with a fork before serving.

....

Tip: Do not stir the rice while it is cooking,
as that can make it gummy.

....

Quinoa

Quinoa often has a coating (called saponin) that imparts a bitter flavor to the seeds once cooked, so rinse and drain quinoa well before cooking.

1 cup quinoa, rinsed and drained

2 cups water

Pinch of sea salt (optional)

Bring all of the ingredients to a boil in a medium pot over high heat. Reduce the heat to low, cover, and simmer until the water is absorbed and the quinoa is tender, about 15 minutes. Fluff up the quinoa with a fork before serving.

Toasting Nuts
& Seeds

Toasting nuts and seeds deepens their flavor and adds color and fragrance. I've found that the quickest way to get the job done is with a clean, dry skillet on the stove. Although nuts toast up well in the oven, too, I'm more likely to forget about and burn them that way, so I use the skillet method most often. Here's how to do it:

1. Place the nuts or seeds in a clean, dry skillet set over medium-high heat.

2. Toast the nuts or seeds, shaking the skillet occasionally, for 3-5 minutes or until lightly browned and fragrant.

3. Cool before using.

A few tips to keep in mind:

🍃 The larger the nut or seed, the longer it will take to toast. For example, walnuts can take up to 5 minutes to get good and toasted, while sesame seeds may be done in 2 minutes or less.

🍃 Pumpkin and sunflower seeds often pop in the skillet as they toast. The more popping you hear, the deeper flavor you're developing.

🍃 Nuts and seeds can go from perfectly golden to bitterly burned in just seconds, so watch them closely!

Pure Menus

Whether you're entertaining, celebrating a holiday or special occasion, or simply in the mood for a fantastic weeknight meal, these pure menus have got you covered. 🍃

All-American Feast

Asian-Style Turkey Burgers with Cucumber Sesame Salad, *page 178*
Sea Salt & Vinegar Kale Chips, *page 108*
Confetti Rice Salad, *page 155*
Banana Coconut Cupcakes with Fudgy Chocolate Frosting, *page 212*

Blissful Brunch

Herb & Heirloom Tomato Frittata, *page 60*
Cinnamon Currant Biscuits, *page 90,* served with jam
Peach, Fennel, & Baby Green Salad, *page 151*

Craving Comfort Food

Meaty Chicken & Mushroom Stew, *page 134*
Mixed Greens with Pears & Grilled Onions, *page 146*
Sweet Potato & Millet Cornbread, *page 94*
Death by Chocolate Cake, *page 216*

Ethnic Favorites

Middle Eastern Marinated Chicken with Warm Tomato Chutney, *page 176*
Lentil Salad with Currants & Mint, *page 154*

Asian-Style Turkey Burgers with Cucumber Sesame Salad, *page 178*
Colorful Coleslaw, *page 147*

Taco Bowls, *page 182*
Two-Step Tortilla Chips, *page 107,* served with Fiesta Guacamole, *page 100*

Healthy Holidays

Crunchy Crackers, *page 105,* served with Fig Spread, *page 104*
Sautéed Chard with Dried Apricots, *page 156*
Maple-Glazed Root Vegetables, *page 158*
Chicken Thighs with Balsamic-Cherry Pan Sauce, *page 174*
Apple Spice Cake with "Caramel" Frosting, *page 218*

Savory Winter Supper

Mini Meatloaves with Chunky Tomato-Basil Sauce, *page 180*
Scallion Smashed Potatoes, *page 161*
Mixed Greens with Pears & Grilled Onions, *page 146*
Dark Chocolate Brownie Balls, *page 203*

Swing into Spring

Cauliflower Parsnip Soup with Spring Pesto Drizzle, *page 128*
Honey Mustard Salmon with Lemony Herbed Quinoa, *page 166*
Lemon Bars with Oatmeal-Coconut Crust, *page 200*

Vegan Feast

Pesto Hummus, *page 102,* served with vegetable crudités
Creamy Kale Salad, *page 144*
Vegan Sloppy Joe Bowls, *page 192*
Two-Bite Raspberry Lemon Tartlets, *page 204*

Warm Weather Fare

Two-Step Tortilla Chips, *page 107,* served with Stone Fruit Salsa, *page 103*
Chicken Strips with Maple-Mustard Dipper, *page 171*
Shredded Balsamic Beet & Kale Salad, *page 148*
Peanut Butter Freezer Treats, *page 202*

With Gratitude

Above all, I am deeply grateful to God and all that He has done in my life. All of my accomplishments, triumphs, and successes I attribute to Him first and always. He has led me and continues to lead me on an incredible journey rich with opportunities and blessings.

To my mom, Carolyn, and my dad, Ray, who taught me the importance of diligence and dedication; instilled in me the desire to be a godly woman of integrity; directed me when I was lost; and encouraged me to believe in myself and my dreams no matter what. Thank you for raising me to be the person I am today.

To my sister, Brianna, who never fails to pick up the phone and call just to say that she's thinking of me and hoping I'm having a good day. She's been my best friend all of my life and influences me every day with her positive, gentle spirit. At the very beginning of this journey, she's the one who urged me to begin writing my blog. From childhood on, our hearts and lives have intertwined only to grow closer over time. Thank you for your love, support, and above all, for simply being there when I need a friend.

To the Winchell family, for sharing countless meals with me and my family, inspiring me to grow deeper in my relationship with God and others, and encouraging me throughout this entire project. Our many years of friendship have shaped a large part of who I am and who I am becoming. Thank you from the bottom of my heart.

To Amy Green, Kelly Brozyna, Alisa Fleming, and Ali Segersten—four amazing women who inspired me to write this book in the first place. The work they do touches the lives of many, including mine. Thank you for all of the emails, phone calls, and pats on the back when I needed them most. My hope is that I can influence others the way you've influenced, motivated, and educated me.

To the online blogging community, for welcoming me when I had no idea what I was doing and taking me under your wing. Thank you for challenging me to grow as a cook and writer, and for giving me daily doses of encouragement, humor, and friendship.

To all of my recipe testers, a big bear hug to each of you! The recipes in this book would not be what they are without your honest, prompt, and thorough feedback. Thank you for taking the time to help me with this project and for your desire to share my perspective on food with the world.

And finally, to the readers of Daily Bites, for coming back week after week and sharing in my little piece of life. You've inspired me, humbled me, cheered me on, and built up my confidence. The day I started writing my blog, I never thought anyone would read it. But you proved me wrong, and I am forever grateful.

About the Author

HALLIE KLECKER authors the gluten-free food blog Daily Bites (www.DailyBitesBlog.com), where she shares her enthusiasm for cooking with whole, natural, unrefined foods. Hallie is also the founder of The Pure Kitchen, a healthy eating coaching service that motivates and supports people on their journey toward wellness and pure living. Hallie offers nutritional coaching, cooking classes, grocery store tours, meal planning assistance, and more to supply individuals with the skills needed to make lasting, positive changes. For more information about The Pure Kitchen, upcoming events, and classes, visit www.InThePureKitchen.com.

After experiencing health issues for several years, Hallie eliminated gluten and dairy from her diet in 2008 and, as a result, has never felt better. Through living free of gluten and dairy and emphasizing pure, unrefined foods in her diet, Hallie has discovered that eating healthfully does not equal boring meals or a pantry stocked with hard-to-find ingredients. A former personal chef, Hallie received her Nutrition Educator Certification from Bauman College of Holistic Nutrition and Culinary Arts and her Personal Chef Certification from the Culinary Business Academy. She lives near Madison, Wisconsin.

Index

www.InThePureKitchen.com

· · · · ·

Made in the USA
Lexington, KY
12 January 2012